Grammar Expert

Series Editors:
Sarah Bideleux
Gill Mackie

Australia • Brazil • Japan • Korea • Mexico • Singapore • Spain • United Kingdom • United States

Grammar Expert Basic
Series Editors: Sarah Bideleux, Gill Mackie

Publisher: Carl Wantenaar
Director of Content Development: Anita Raducanu
International Marketing Manager: Ian Martin
Production Project Manager: Natasa Arsenidou
Print Buyer: Marybeth Hennebury
Compositor: Vasiliki Christoforides
Project Manager: Diane Flanel Piniaris
Contributing Writers: Francesca Stafford, Nicholas Stephens
Consulting Editor: James W. Brown
Illustrators: Ilias Sounas, Katerina Chrysochoou
Cover/Text Designer: Sophia Fourtouni, Natasa Arsenidou

Cover image: www.photos.com

© 2007 Heinle, Cengage Learning

ALL RIGHTS RESERVED. No part of this work covered by the copyright herein may be reproduced, transmitted, stored or used in any form or by any means graphic, electronic, or mechanical, including but not limited to photocopying, recording, scanning, digitizing, taping, Web distribution, information networks, or information storage and retrieval systems, except as permitted under Section 107 or 108 of the 1976 United States Copyright Act, without the prior written permission of the publisher.

For product information and technology assistance, contact us at
Cengage Learning Customer & Sales Support, 1-800-354-9706
For permission to use material from this text or product, submit all requests online at **cengage.com/permissions**
Further permissions questions can be emailed to
permissionrequest@cengage.com

ISBN-13: 978-960-403-288-4

ISBN-10: 960-403-288-7

Heinle
20 Channel Center
Boston, MA 02210
USA

Cengage Learning is a leading provider of customized learning solutions with office locations around the globe, including Singapore, the United Kingdom, Australia, Mexico, Brazil, and Japan. Locate your local office at:
international.cengage.com/region

Cengage Learning products are represented in Canada by Nelson Education, Ltd.

Visit Heinle online at **elt.heinle.com**

Visit our corporate website at **www.cengage.com**

Printed in China by China Translation & Printing Services Limited
2 3 4 5 6 7 8 9 10 14 13 12 11

Contents

1	Subject Pronouns & Simple Present: To Be	*page 4*
2	Articles, Regular & Irregular Plurals	*page 8*
3	Prepositions of Place & There Is / There Are	*page 12*
4	Simple Present: To Have	*page 15*
	REVIEW 1	*page 18*
5	Possessive Adjectives & Pronouns, 's, Demonstratives & Who's / Whose?	*page 22*
6	Simple Present, Adverbs of Frequency & Prepositions of Time	*page 26*
7	Adverbs, Too & Enough	*page 31*
8	Present Continuous	*page 34*
	REVIEW 2	*page 38*
9	Simple Present & Present Continuous	*page 42*
10	Can & Must	*page 46*
11	Imperative, Let's & Object Pronouns	*page 50*
12	Simple Past: To Be	*page 53*
	REVIEW 3	*page 56*
13	Simple Past Affirmative: Regular & Irregular Verbs	*page 60*
14	Simple Past Negative & Question	*page 64*
15	Some, Any, No, Every	*page 67*
16	Count & Noncount Nouns & Quantifiers	*page 70*
	REVIEW 4	*page 74*
17	Adjectives: Comparatives and Superlatives	*page 78*
18	Be Going To & the Future with Will	*page 82*
19	Question Words	*page 86*
20	Present Perfect: Regular and Irregular Verbs	*page 90*
	REVIEW 5	*page 94*
	IRREGULAR VERBS	*page 98*

1 Subject Pronouns & Simple Present: To Be

Subject Pronouns

Singular	Plural
I	we
you	you
he	they
she	
it	

Subject pronouns take the place of a subject noun in a sentence.
John is sick today. He is not at work.

We use *it* for things or animals. But if the animal is our pet, we often use *he* or *she*.
Listen to the music. It's very loud.
I like my cat. She's beautiful.

We use *you* for the singular and the plural.
You are tired, Maria.
You are tired, John and Sarah.

We use *they* for two or more people, animals or things.
How are your children? They're fine.
Are cats good pets? Yes, they are.
When are the exams? They're in May.

1 Write the subject pronouns.

Ex. Aunt Mary .... *she* ....

1 the bag ....
2 Anne ....
3 my father ....
4 my mother ....
5 Jane and Tim ....
6 my friend and I ....
7 the book ....
8 the chairs ....

2 Complete the sentences with subject pronouns.

Ex. .... *We* .... are happy today. (Mike and I)

1 .... are in the park. (the dogs)
2 .... isn't my daughter. (Susan)
3 .... are neighbors. (Tom and you)
4 .... is late for work. (John)
5 .... is in my bag. (the report)
6 .... are on vacation. (my wife and I)
7 .... aren't at home today. (the children)
8 .... are at the movies. (Kevin and Lisa)

4

Subject Pronouns & Simple Present: To Be 1

Simple Present: To Be

Affirmative
I am (I'm)
you are (you're)
he is (he's)
she is (she's)
it is (it's)
we are (we're)
you are (you're)
they are (they're)

Negative
I am not (I'm not)
you are not (you aren't / you're not)
he is not (he isn't / he's not)
she is not (she isn't / she's not)
it is not (it isn't / it's not)
we are not (we aren't / we're not)
you are not (you aren't / you're not)
they are not (they aren't / they're not)

Question
Am I?
Are you?
Is he?
Is she?
Is it?
Are we?
Are you?
Are they?

We use *to be* to talk about someone's job, nationality, relationship or name.
He is a lawyer.
We are German.
She is my cousin.
I am Peter.

We also use *to be* to describe people and things.
She is tall.
The sky is gray.

In everyday English we often use short forms.
Hello. I'm Jenny.
He's a doctor.

Short Answers

Yes, I am.
Yes, you are.
Yes, he is.
Yes, she is.
Yes, it is.
Yes, we are.
Yes, you are.
Yes, they are.

No, I'm not.
No, you aren't. / No, you're not.
No, he isn't. / No, he's not.
No, she isn't. / No, she's not.
No, it isn't. / No, it's not.
No, we aren't. / No, we're not.
No, you aren't. / No, you're not.
No, they aren't. / No, they're not.

---

3 Complete the sentences with the Simple Present of *to be*
(✓ = affirmative; ✗ = negative).

Ex.   She .... *is* .... very hungry. ✓

1   The shop .... next to our house. ✓

2   The book .... in the office. ✗

3   I .... thirsty. ✗

4   The plates .... on the table. ✗

5   The flowers .... very pretty. ✓

6   You .... very good at your job. ✓

7   She .... here today. ✗

8   Rebecca and Michael .... bored. ✓

4 Choose the correct answer.

Ex.   *Is* (he) / *they at work?*

1   *She / I* isn't in the bedroom.
2   *They / She* are Mexican.
3   *We / He* aren't in the kitchen.
4   *She / I* is at work.
5   *They / She* are busy.
6   *We / She* are sleepy.
7   Is *you / he* sad?
8   Are *you / it* doctors?

5

1

5 ▸ Complete the questions with **am**, **are** or **is**. Then write short answers: ✓ = Yes; ✗ = No.

Ex. *Is* .... it cold today? ✓
Yes, it is.

1 .... dinner ready? ✗
....

2 .... I tall? ✓
....

3 .... they at the gym? ✓
....

4 .... we at the new office? ✓
....

5 .... the children outside? ✗
....

6 .... the laptop on the desk? ✓
....

Think about it

We do not use short forms of **to be** in affirmative short answers.

7 .... the pens in the briefcase? ✗
....

8 .... she at the office? ✓
....

Simple Present of To Be: Negative Questions

Negative Questions
Aren't I?
Aren't you?
Isn't he?
Isn't she?
Isn't it?
Aren't we?
Aren't you?
Aren't they?

We often use negative questions when we expect the answer: "Yes."
Isn't it cold today?
Yes, it is. It's freezing.

6 ▸ Complete the questions with **aren't** or **isn't**.

Ex. ....*Isn't*........ the food good?

1 .... she with the boss?

2 .... the computers new?

3 .... I good at my job?

4 .... it great news?

5 .... he happy with his job?

6 .... you ready to go?

7 .... they French?

8 .... he the manager of the company?

7 ▸ Rewrite the sentences with subject pronouns.

Ex. *Is the dog hungry?*
Is it hungry?

1 Maria is on vacation this week.
....

2 Sue and Paul aren't at home.
....

3 Tim and I are doctors.
....

4 Are the children asleep?
....

5 Isn't Peter a good singer?
....

6 Is Mr. Jones at work today?
....

8 Write sentences or questions with **to be**.

Ex. she / be / very tall
     She is very tall.

1 you / be / late / for the meeting / ?

2 I / not be / ready for work

3 she / be / at the library now

4 our friends / not be / at the beach

5 the lake / be / full of boats

6 you / be / ready / for lunch / ?

7 you / be / sleepy / ?

8 the glasses / be / on your desk

9 Complete the text with **is, isn't, are or aren't**.

(Ex.) ......*Is*...... Martin sad today? Yes, he (1) .... It (2) .... a cold day and the sky (3) .... gray. It (4) .... Monday and Martin (5) .... on vacation. He (6) .... at work. His friends (7) .... on vacation together. They (8) .... in the office. They (9) .... in Japan. They (10) .... at their favorite golf course.

Pairwork

Work with a partner. Take turns. Ask and answer the following questions:

➤ Is it rainy today?
➤ Are you tired?
➤ Are you at work now?
➤ Is the weather bad today?
➤ Are you hungry?
➤ Is it dinner time?
➤ Is grammar difficult?
➤ Is English interesting?

Writing

Write a short paragraph. Answer these questions:

➤ How is the weather today?
➤ Where are you now?
➤ Where are your friends?

2 Articles, Regular & Irregular Plurals

The Indefinite Article

a
a boy
a pen
a house
a garden
a tree
a uniform
a brown ball
a red apple
a beautiful morning

an
an ant
an egg
an elephant
an island
an owl
an umbrella
an hour
an interesting book
an exciting story
an orange jacket

We use the indefinite articles *a* and *an* with singular nouns.
a book   *an airplane*

We use *a* before a consonant sound (*b, c, d, f, g, h, j, k, l, m, n, p, q, r, s, t, v, w, x, y, z*) and *an* before a vowel sound (*a, e, i, o, u*).
a pen   *an elephant*

Sometimes there is an adjective before the noun. When the adjective begins with a consonant sound, we use *a*. When it begins with a vowel sound, we use *an*.
a red apple   *an exciting story*

We use *a* or *an* to talk about one person, animal or thing in general. (We don't use *a* or *an* to talk about someone or something specific.)
A computer is on the desk.   There is a movie on television.

Notes

Be careful with words that begin with *h* or *u*. When the word begins with a consonant sound, we use *a*. When the word begins with a vowel sound, we use *an*.
a hat, a hospital, a hotel, a unit, a university, a uniform
an hour, an umbrella, an uncle

1 Write a or an.

Ex. ......*an*...... egg

1 .... airplane
2 .... project
3 .... computer
4 .... apple
5 .... desk
6 .... briefcase
7 .... animal
8 .... hospital
9 .... ant
10 .... evening
11 .... uniform
12 .... kite

8

Articles, Regular & Irregular Plurals 2

2 ▶ Write **a** or **an**.

Ex. ......*a*...... *small globe*

1 .... polite person
2 .... orange box
3 .... awful vacation
4 .... good worker
5 .... long road
6 .... blue umbrella
7 .... exciting project
8 .... large meal
9 .... interesting job
10 .... university degree
11 .... big ice cream
12 .... old woman

The Definite Article

the
The Earth is round.
The Mediterranean Sea is beautiful.
The reports are on the desk.

We use the definite article *the*:

➤ to talk about specific people, things or animals (singular or plural).
The dog is in the yard.
The manager is in the cafeteria.

➤ to talk about something that is unique.
The moon is full tonight.

➤ with the names of mountain ranges (*the Alps*), oceans (*the Atlantic Ocean*) and seas (*the Arabian Sea*), rivers (*the Amazon*) and deserts (*the Sahara Desert*).

➤ with musical instruments.
The piano is in the living room.

We don't use *the*:

➤ with people's names.
Jane and Marina are sisters.

➤ with the names of most countries. (But we say: *the United States, the Netherlands,* etc.)
Italy is a lovely country.

➤ with subjects, games or sports.
Physics and chemistry are difficult subjects.
Chess is an interesting game.
Basketball is my favorite sport.

➤ when the noun is plural and we are talking about people, animals or things in general.
Theater tickets are expensive.
Lions are dangerous animals.

3 ▶ Complete the sentences with **a, an** or **the**.

Ex. ......*An*...... *orange bicycle and* ......*a*...... *red car are outside* ......*the*...... *house.*

1 There's .... report on your desk. .... report is 15 pages.
2 This is Norman's desk. On .... desk is .... reading lamp and .... laptop computer.
3 Berlin is .... fantastic place. .... downtown area is exciting, and .... parks of Berlin are huge!
4 Look! .... old man and .... dog are in .... street.

9

2

4 ▸ Complete the sentences with **the** or – (for no article).

Ex.   ....*The*.... Amazon is in South America.

1 Ella and Betty are on a hiking vacation in .... Rocky Mountains.
2 Is .... mathematics a difficult subject for you?
3 .... Rio Grande is a big river between .... United States and .... Mexico.
4 Amsterdam is in .... Netherlands.
5 .... Danube is a big river in Europe.
6 Fran plays .... guitar.
7 .... Mount Fuji is in .... Japan, and .... Mount Pinatubo is in .... Philippines.
8 .... Eiffel Tower is in .... Paris.

Regular Plurals

Singular	Plural
boy	boys
bus	buses
brush	brushes
pencil	pencils
dress	dresses
watch	watches
fox	foxes
photo	photos
tomato	tomatoes
wife	wives
leaf	leaves
party	parties

We usually make a noun plural by adding -s.
book → books
chair → chairs

We add -es to words that end in -s, -ss, -sh, -ch and -x.
bus → buses
box → boxes

When a word ends in a consonant and -y, we take off the -y and add -ies.
lady → ladies

When a word ends in a vowel and -y, we just add -s.
day → days
key → keys

We usually add -s to words that end in -o. Sometimes we add -es.
piano → pianos
photo → photos
tomato → tomatoes
potato → potatoes

When a word ends in -f or -fe, we usually take off the -f or -fe and add -ves. But we just add -s to the words *giraffe* and *roof*.
wife → wives
half → halves
giraffe → giraffes
roof → roofs

Irregular plurals do not follow any rules. You must learn them.

Irregular Plurals

Singular	Plural
person	people
child	children
man	men
woman	women
foot	feet
tooth	teeth
mouse	mice
sheep	sheep
deer	deer
goose	geese
ox	oxen

5 ▸ Write the plurals.

Ex. book   ....*books*....

1 wife   ....
2 violin   ....
3 idea   ....
4 potato   ....
5 watch   ....

6 story   ....
7 fox   ....
8 wish   ....
9 loaf   ....
10 cherry   ....

Think about it

We say **one** instead of **an** when we are counting.

10

Articles, Regular & Irregular Plurals 2

6 Write the plurals.

Ex. deer .... *deer* ....

1 goose ....
2 mouse ....
3 man ....
4 tooth ....
5 sheep ....
6 person ....
7 child ....
8 foot ....
9 woman ....
10 ox ....

7 Complete the sentences with the plural of the words in parentheses.

Ex. Rover and Spot are .... *dogs* .... (dog)

1 Look! Six .... are in that car! (person)
2 Her .... aren't white; they're yellow. (tooth)
3 The two .... are good friends. (man)
4 Are the .... in the city new? (bus)
5 My .... are small. (foot)
6 The .... in this shop aren't expensive. (dress)
7 Two hundred .... are on Tim's farm. (sheep)
8 .... are very noisy animals. (goose)
9 Are the .... on the kitchen table? (sandwich)
10 Are .... good for you? (tomato)

Pairwork

Work with a partner. Think of a river, a country, a famous hotel and a mountain range. Ask your partner where they are. Now change roles.

Writing

Write a list of the things in your living room, your bedroom or your English class.

11

3 Prepositions of Place & There Is / There Are

Prepositions of Place

at
behind
between
in
in front of
near
next to
on
under

We use prepositions of place to show where something or someone is. The most common prepositions of place are:

➤ **at**
They are at the office.

➤ **behind**
The shop is behind the school.

➤ **between**
Our office is between the bakery and the bank.

➤ **in**
The food is in the oven.

➤ **in front of**
The bag is in front of the desk.

➤ **near**
They are near the station.

➤ **next to**
My house is next to the park.

➤ **on**
The hat is on the floor.

➤ **under**
The cat is under the table.

1 Complete the sentences with the words in the box.

| behind | between | ~~in~~ | in front of | next to | on | under |

Ex. The address book is ......*in*...... the briefcase.

1 The address book is .... the phone.

2 The address book is .... the desk.

3 The address book is .... the briefcase.

4 The address book is .... the briefcase.

5 The address book is .... the phone.

6 The address book is .... the phone and the briefcase.

12

Prepositions of Place & There Is / There Are 3

At, In, On

Here are some useful phrases with prepositions of place.

at	in	on
at the top	in the hospital	on the left/right
at the bottom	in a car	on the wall
at school	in bed	on the plane/train/bus
at work	in the middle	on the ground
at the office	in an armchair	on a chair/sofa/couch
at home	in the sky	on television/radio

2 Find the mistakes and write the sentences correctly.

Ex. *Jane isn't in home this morning.*
Jane isn't at home this morning.

1 There is a computer in the desk.
   ....

2 They aren't on work today.
   ....

3 There is a glass at the table.
   ....

4 There is a mouse at the kitchen.
   ....

5 There are strange animals in the bottom of the sea.
   ....

6 My friends are in the train now.
   ....

7 The desk is on the middle of the office.
   ....

8 It's cold in the top of the mountain.
   ....

There Is / There Are

Affirmative
there is (there's)
there are

Negative
there is not (there isn't)
there are not (there aren't)

Question
Is there?
Are there?

We use *there is* and *there are* to talk or ask about what exists when we are describing something in the present.
There is a computer on the desk.
There are 150 employees in the building.
There isn't a movie on TV tonight.
Are there three meetings today?

Short Answers
Yes, there is.   No, there isn't.
Yes, there are.   No, there aren't.

3 Choose the correct answer.

Ex. There is / (There are) *two managers in my office.*

1 There is / There are twenty people in the bank.
2 There is / There are a police station in my town.
3 There is / There are wild animals in the jungle.
4 There is / There are two bicycles in the garage.
5 There is / There are only one basketball team here.
6 There is / There are a new e-mail in my inbox.
7 There is / There are a difficult exercise in my book.
8 There is / There are five dogs in my neighborhood.

13

3

4 ▶ Write short answers.

Ex. *Is there a bag on the table?* ✓
Yes, there is.

1 Is there a glass of juice on the table? ✗
....
2 Are there cats in your house? ✓
....
3 Is there a photocopier in your office? ✓
....
4 Are there people in the building? ✗
....
5 Is there a book in your bag? ✗
....

5 ▶ Write questions.

Ex. sofa / in / living room / ?
Is there a sofa in the living room?

1 phone / in / office / ?
....
2 chicken / in / garden / ?
....
3 bag / next to / chair / ?
....
4 restaurants / near / office / ?
....
5 cats / under / bed / ?
....

6 ▶ Complete the text with the words in the box.

> between   ~~in~~   is   middle   near (x2)   on   there (x2)

(Ex.) ....*In*........ my neighborhood (1) .... is a lovely park. In the (2) .... of the park, (3) .... is a fountain and two statues. (4) .... the two statues there is a bench. Behind the bench there (5) .... a large tree. (6) .... the ground under the tree, there are five birds. (7) .... the tree is a high fence. The parking lot is (8) .... the fence.

Pairwork

Work with a partner. Ask and answer questions about your favorite place. Use prepositions of place and *there is / there are*.

Writing

Write a letter to a friend. Describe your house. Use prepositions of place and *there is / there are*.

Dear ....,
....
....
....
....
....
....
....
....

Your friend,
....

14

Simple Present: To Have   4

Simple Present: To Have

Affirmative	Negative	Question
I have	I do not (don't) have	Do I have?
you have	you do not (don't) have	Do you have?
he has	he does not (doesn't) have	Does he have?
she has	she does not (doesn't) have	Does she have?
it has	it does not (doesn't) have	Does it have?
we have	we do not (don't) have	Do we have?
you have	you do not (don't) have	Do you have?
they have	they do not (don't) have	Do they have?

Short Answers

Yes, I do.   No, I don't.
Yes, you do.   No, you don't.
Yes, he does.   No, he doesn't.
Yes, she does.   No, she doesn't.
Yes, it does.   No, it doesn't.
Yes, we do.   No, we don't.
Yes, you do.   No, you don't.
Yes, they do.   No, they don't.

We use *to have*:

➤ to show that something belongs to someone.
We have a car.

➤ to describe a person, thing or animal.
The twins have brown eyes.

➤ to talk about a physical problem.
I have a headache.

Unlike *to be*, with *to have* and other verbs in the Simple Present, we use the auxiliary *do/does* in negatives, questions and short answers. Use *does* with *he*, *she* and *it*. Use *do* with all other forms.

Does he have short hair?
No, he doesn't have short hair.

Do you have a new car?
Yes, I do. / No, I don't.

---

1 Complete the sentences with the Simple Present of **to have**.

Ex. She ....*has*........ a nice brother.

1 You .... the report on your desk.
2 They .... a dog and two cats.
3 He .... a nice house.
4 I .... allergies.
5 We .... two children.
6 It .... two big windows.

2 Complete the sentences with the negative form of the Simple Present of **to have**.

Ex. They ....*don't have*............ a dictionary.

1 She .... a headache.
2 The building .... an elevator.
3 I .... time to finish this work.
4 We .... the keys.
5 Kim .... a nice jacket.
6 You .... dark hair.

15

4

3 Complete the questions with **to have** and the words in parentheses.

Ex. *Do you have* .... my phone number? (you)
1. .... a fever? (I)
2. .... a car? (your friend)
3. .... blue eyes? (you)
4. .... a new dress? (Sylvia)
5. .... a tennis racket? (he)
6. .... a credit card? (they)
7. .... children? (your daughter)
8. .... tall buildings? (New York City)

4 Answer the questions. Give extra information if you can.

Ex. *Do you have long hair?*
No, I don't. I have short hair.

1. Do you have a computer?
   ....
2. Do you have brown eyes?
   ....
3. Do you have a car?
   ....
4. Do you have a passport?
   ....
5. Do you have a pet?
   ....
6. Do you have a cold?
   ....

5 Look at the chart. Then write questions and answers.

Judy has . . .	Mike and Chris have . . .
a new puppy	new bicycles
an old car	laptops
orange sandals	short hair
long hair	a DVD player
a big yard	a black cat

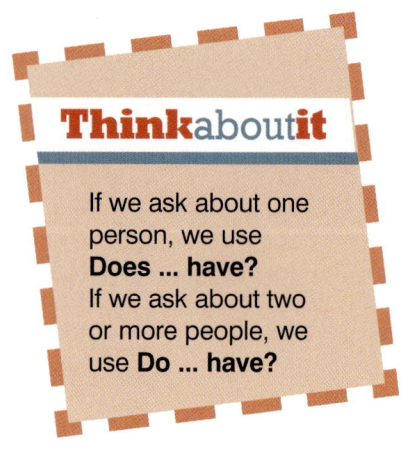

Thinkabout**it**

If we ask about one person, we use **Does ... have?** If we ask about two or more people, we use **Do ... have?**

Ex. *Mike and Chris / a new puppy / ?*
Do Mike and Chris have a new puppy?
No, they don't. Judy has a new puppy.

1. Judy / a new bicycle / ?
   ....
2. Judy / a laptop / ?
   ....
3. Mike and Chris / long hair / ?
   ....
4. Judy / orange sandals / ?
   ....
5. Mike and Chris / old car / ?
   ....
6. Mike and Chris / a DVD player / ?
   ....
7. Judy / a black cat / ?
   ....
8. Mike and Chris / a big yard / ?
   ....

Simple Present: To Have 4

6 Complete the text with the Simple Present of *to be* or *to have*.

My name (Ex.) ......*is*...... Sheila. My friend Jane and I (1) .... jobs at the Big Business Computer Company in Chicago. I (2) .... a computer programmer and Jane (3) .... a job in the Sales Department. Jane and her boss (4) .... an office with a great view of the lake. Jane and I (5) .... roommates, too. We (6) .... an apartment on Lake View Avenue. It (7) .... a big place with two bedrooms and a great kitchen. We always (8) .... fun together.

7 Write questions and short answers with *to be* or *to have*.

Ex. cold day / ? ✓
Is it a cold day?   Yes, it is.

1 Penny / good employee / ? ✓

2 Mary / a new job / ? ✗

3 the employees / on time for work / ? ✗

4 there / a tree / behind the house / ? ✗

5 Jerry and Martha / new baby / ? ✓

6 you and John / plants / in the house / ? ✓

7 Diane and Rita / on vacation / now / ? ✓

8 I / time / for a cup of coffee / ? ✗

Think about it

What differences do you see in questions and answers with **be** and questions and answers with **have**?

Is he a good driver?
Yes, he is.

Does he have a new car?
No, he doesn't.

Pairwork

Work with a partner. Ask and answer questions with *have*. Find out five things your partner *has* and five things he or she *doesn't have*.

Writing

Write a paragraph about your partner. Think about:
➤ what he/she has.
➤ what he/she doesn't have.

Review 1 (Units 1-4)

1 Complete the sentences with the Simple Present of to be.

Ex. She ....*is*........ very tired. ✓

1 My car .... very old. ✓
2 Her job .... interesting. ✗
3 The books .... very expensive. ✗
4 Claire and Jane .... sisters. ✓

5 It .... warm today. ✗
6 He .... a great golf player. ✓
7 I .... hungry this evening. ✗
8 The children .... noisy. ✓

2 Complete the questions with am, are or is and write answers.

Ex. *Is*........ it raining today? ✓
   Yes, it is..................

1 .... your presentation good? ✓
   ....
2 .... he at home? ✓
   ....
3 .... we at your office? ✗
   ....
4 .... the children at school? ✗
   ....

5 .... you alone? ✓
   ....
6 .... the ideas good? ✗
   ....
7 .... the jacket expensive? ✓
   ....
8 .... you hungry? ✓
   ....

3 Choose the correct answer.

Ex. Is (she) / they interesting?

1 They / He is unhappy.
2 Are she / they playing basketball?
3 We / He are in the office.
4 He / I isn't at work.

5 I / She am a manager.
6 Are you / he smart?
7 We / I are thirsty.
8 He / I is at home.

4 Write sentences or questions with to be.

Ex. he / not be / boring
   He isn't boring...

1 our children / be / at school today
   ....
2 the boss / be / angry today / ?
   ....
3 Michael / be / polite
   ....
4 Professor Lee / not be / in his office
   ....

5 you / sad / today / ?
   ....
6 the meeting / be / interesting
   ....
7 he / not be / an honest person
   ....
8 the boxes / be / in the car
   ....

Review 1 (Units 1-4)

5 Put the words in the correct part of the chart.

adventure story   awful book   blue pen   ~~box~~   car   dog   elephant   English lesson
great idea   happy person   honest man   interesting job   island   orange   pineapple   rainy day

a	an
box	*elephant*

6 Write the plurals.

	Singular	Plural
Ex.	leaf	*leaves*
1	watch	....
2	tooth	....
3	photo	....
4	sheep	....
5	man	....
6	bus	....
7	fox	....
8	brush	....
9	woman	....
10	boy	....
11	person	....
12	child	....
13	mouse	....
14	foot	....
15	party	....

7 Complete the sentences with **there is** or **there are**.

Ex. ....*There are*........ two oranges on the table.
1 .... three children in the street.
2 .... a bird on my car.
3 .... a bank near the office.
4 .... ten students in our English class.
5 .... a great pizza place on the corner.
6 .... lots of apples on the tree.
7 .... two windows in my bedroom.
8 .... a cat at my front door.

19

Review 1

8 Write questions and answers with **there is** or **there are**.

Ex. a cat / in / the basket / ? ✓
Is there a cat in the basket?
Yes, there is.

1 books / in / the bag / ? ✓
....
....

2 three pens / on / the desk / ? ✗
....
....

3 a large building / next to / your office / ? ✗
....
....

4 a yellow hat / on / the table / ? ✓
....
....

5 plates / in / the sink / ? ✗
....
....

6 a lamp / in / the kitchen / ? ✓
....
....

7 a cat / in / the garden / ? ✓
....
....

8 beaches / near / the city / ? ✓
....
....

9 Find the mistakes and write the sentences correctly.

Ex. *My sister is in work today.*
My sister is at work today.

1 The cat is on the bedroom.
....
....

2 The students are not on class this week.
....
....

3 There are two boys in the bus stop.
....
....

4 It's the house in the left.
....
....

5 The children are at bed.
....
....

6 The picture is at the wall.
....
....

7 Eric is in home.
....
....

8 The starfish is in the bottom of the ocean.
....
....

Review 1 (Units 1-4)

10 ▸ **Complete the sentences with prepositions of place.**

Ex. *The books are ......next to...... the desk.*

1   The books are .... the desk.
2   The books are .... the desk.
3   The books are .... the desk.
4   The books are .... the two desks.
5   The books are .... the desk.

Ex.

1

2

3

4

5

11 ▸ **Complete the sentences with the Simple Present of to have.**

Ex. *I ....have........ a new car.* ✓

1   I .... a toothache. ✓
2   We .... a lot of work to do. ✗
3   They .... a nice house. ✓
4   I .... a new job. ✗
5   You .... a motorcycle. ✓
6   She .... a cell phone. ✗
7   They .... a new car. ✗
8   We .... a great camera. ✓

12 ▸ **Complete the questions with the correct form of to have and the words in parentheses.**

Ex. ......*Do you have*...... *a pen? (you)*

1   .... the book I want? (Sarah)
2   .... presents for their friends? (they)
3   .... a DVD recorder? (you)
4   .... a driver's licence? (Mark)
5   .... brown eyes? (your daughter)
6   .... friends in Canada? (you)
7   .... time for a cup of coffee? (we)
8   .... a broken leg? (the man)

21

5 Possessive Adjectives & Pronouns, 's, Demonstratives & Who's / Whose?

Possessive Adjectives

Subject Pronouns	Possessive Adjectives
I	my
you	your
he	his
she	her
it	its
we	our
you	your
they	their

We use possessive adjectives when:

➤ something belongs to someone.
That's his bag.

➤ someone has a particular relationship with someone or something.
Jake is my friend.

1 Complete the sentences with possessive adjectives.

Ex. ......*My*...... friend is at home. (I)

1 .... water is in the bowl. (it)
2 .... package is on the table. (you)
3 .... garden is very large. (they)
4 .... milk is on the table. (you)
5 .... house is next to the café. (he)
6 .... keys are at home. (I)
7 .... cousin works with me. (she)
8 .... house is large. (we)

Think about it

The possessive adjective **its** does not have an apostrophe. **It's** means **it is**.

22

Possessive Adjectives & Pronouns, 's, Demonstratives & Who's / Whose? 5

Possessive 's

We use 's to show that something belongs to someone.
This is Maria's pen.

We add 's to names or to singular nouns.
Jenny's sister has a good job.
The girl's sister has a good job.

When the noun is plural, the apostrophe comes after the s.
The girls' sisters have good jobs.

When the noun has an irregular plural, we add 's.
The women's sisters have good jobs.

2 Complete the sentences with the possessive 's ('s or ') and the words in parentheses.

Ex. ......*Emma's*...... office is near the stadium. (Emma)

1 .... house is in the mountains. (Roger)
2 My .... name is Maria. (friend)
3 The .... cat is friendly. (girls)
4 The .... company is in New York. (man)
5 Their .... name is Smith. (boss)
6 My .... names are John and George. (brothers)
7 His .... family is Mexican. (mother)
8 My .... school is near the post office. (children)

Possessive Pronouns

Possessive Adjectives	Possessive Pronouns
my	mine
your	yours
his	his
her	hers
its	–
our	ours
your	your
their	theirs

We use possessive pronouns when something belongs to someone or when someone has a particular relationship with something.
The car is mine.

After a possessive adjective, there is always a noun. But a possessive pronoun replaces a possessive adjective and a noun.
It's my car. It's mine.
It's her house. It's hers.

3 Complete the sentences with possessive pronouns.

Ex. The DVD is ......*mine*...... . (I)

1 The green book is .... (he)
2 The computer is .... (she)
3 This cup of tea is .... (you)
4 The bicycles are .... (they)
5 That car is .... (we)
6 The idea is .... (you)

6 Simple Present, Adverbs of Frequency & Prepositions of Time

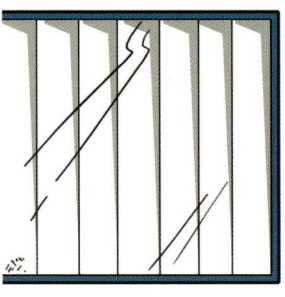

HE DOESN'T USUALLY DANCE ON MONDAY MORNINGS.

Simple Present

Affirmative
I work
you work
he works
she works
it works
we work
you work
they work

Negative
I do not (don't) work
you do not (don't) work
he does not (doesn't) work
she does not (doesn't) work
it does not (doesn't) work
we do not (don't) work
you do not (don't) work
they do not (don't) work

Question
Do I work?
Do you work?
Does he work?
Does she work?
Does it work?
Do we work?
Do you work?
Do they work?

Short Answers

Yes, I do.	No, I don't.
Yes, you do.	No, you don't.
Yes, he does.	No, he doesn't.
Yes, she does.	No, she doesn't.
Yes, it does.	No, it doesn't.
Yes, we do.	No, we don't.
Yes, you do.	No, you don't.
Yes, they do.	No, they don't.

We use the Simple Present to talk about:

➤ permanent states.
My brother works in Tokyo.

➤ things we do often.
She visits her sister every week.

➤ general truths.
It rains a lot in Seattle.

In the third person singular affirmative (*he, she, it*), we add *-s* to the verb.
run ➜ runs
work ➜ works

We add *-es* to verbs which end in *-ss, -sh, -ch, -x* and *-o* in the third person singular affirmative.
miss ➜ misses
crash ➜ crashes
match ➜ matches
mix ➜ mixes
go ➜ goes

When a verb ends in a consonant + *-y*, we take off the *-y* and add *-ies* in the third person singular affirmative.
fly ➜ flies
carry ➜ carries

When a verb ends in a vowel + *-y*, we just add *-s* in the third person singular affirmative.
buy ➜ buys

In the negative and question forms, we use the auxiliary verb *do/does* and the base form of the main verb.
She doesn't like David.
We don't go out on Friday night.
Do they play tennis?
Does Jane live in Panama?

In short answers, we only use *do/does*. We don't use the main verb.
Do they enjoy classical music? Yes, they do.
Does she play the violin? No, she doesn't.

Simple Present, Adverbs of Frequency & Prepositions of Time 6

1 Complete the chart.

Verb	Third Person Singular
stay	stays
miss	
fly	
know	
fix	
do	
watch	
buy	
wash	

2 Complete the sentences with the negative form of the Simple Present.

Ex. I .... *don't eat* .... fish. (eat)

1 They .... to college. (go)
2 He .... orange juice. (drink)
3 We .... classical music. (like)
4 She .... Spanish. (speak)
5 You .... my friend. (know)
6 I .... expensive clothes. (buy)
7 She .... at my jokes. (laugh)
8 He .... history. (teach)

3 Complete the questions with the Simple Present and write answers.

Ex. *Do you watch* old movies? (you / watch) ✓
    Yes, I do.

1 .... my name? (he / remember) ✓
   ....
2 .... Chinese food? (they / like) ✗
   ....
3 .... nice? (I / look) ✓
   ....
4 .... chess? (she / play) ✗
   ....
5 .... computer programs? (he / write) ✓
   ....
6 .... a lot of money? (they / spend) ✗
   ....
7 .... a big company? (that man / own) ✓
   ....
8 .... Spanish? (your friend / Spanish) ✗
   ....

Adverbs of Frequency

When we talk about habits or we want to say how often something happens, we use adverbs of frequency. Some common adverbs of frequency are:

never	sometimes	often / usually	always
0%			100%

In the Simple Present, adverbs of frequency usually come after the verb *to be* and before all other main verbs.
I am never late for an appointment.
He often plays tennis.

Time expressions such as *every day, every week, once a week* and *on Monday(s)* usually go at the beginning or the end of a sentence.
She runs in the park every morning.
On Sundays we watch DVDs.

6

4 Write the words in the correct order.

Ex. *he / his parents / misses / often*
He often misses his parents.

1 early / they / for meetings / always / are
....

2 Jason / buys / sometimes / shirts
....

3 goes / Peter / never / by bus / to work
....

4 goes / sometimes / she / to the theater
....

5 Jessica / our mistakes / often / corrects
....

6 usually / I / not / have / at this time / lunch / do
....

7 late / he / often / is / ?
....

8 not / our friends / go running / do / often
....

Prepositions of Time

at
at 8 o'clock
at night
at noon
at lunchtime
at dinnertime

in
in the morning
in the afternoon
in the evening
in 2002
in the summer
in May

on
on Sundays
on Tuesday mornings
on June 6th
on my birthday
on New Year's Day
on New Year's Eve

5 Complete the sentences with **at**, **in** or **on**.

Ex. He always goes to the gym .... *at* .... noon.

1 We always have dinner .... 7 o'clock.
2 He visits his parents .... Sundays.
3 I have a guitar lesson .... 8 o'clock .... the evening.
4 They like the snow .... the winter.
5 They usually go to the mall .... Saturday afternoons.
6 Her birthday is .... July 6th.
7 He runs .... the morning.
8 They get up late .... Sunday mornings and go for a walk.
9 Does she do her homework .... night?
10 I never invite people to my house .... my birthday.

6 Write sentences with the Simple Present.

Ex. *George / see / his friends / Sundays*
George sees his friends on Sundays.

1 they / not clean / the office / Mondays
....

2 Jamie / always / play / tennis / Saturday
....

3 her sister / always / cook / evening / ?
....

4 Ed / have / party / New Year's Eve
....

5 she / usually / call / her mother / the morning
....

6 they / sometimes / go on vacation / June
....

28

Simple Present, Adverbs of Frequency & Prepositions of Time 6

7 Write the words in the correct order.

Ex. *often / writes / she / to a friend / e-mails*
She often writes e-mails to a friend.

1 Sundays / eat at home / they / never / on
....

2 January / travels / usually / she / in / to London / with her friends
....

3 they / in the lake / swim / do / often / ?
....

4 play / the / doesn't / in / he / chess / morning
....

5 sometimes / have lunch / I / with my boss
....

6 see / she / on / doesn't / her friends / evenings / usually / Wednesday
....

8 Complete the sentences with one word in each blank.

Ex. *Peter does not go to bed at the same time ......every...... evening.*

1 I .... not put salt on my food.
2 We have a meeting .... Tuesdays.
3 We have fun .... evening.
4 .... his cousin work in the same office?
5 They do .... always go swimming in the summer.
6 The weather is terrible .... the winter.
7 Paul .... not like cheese.
8 Do you go to the movies .... Saturday night?

9 Find the mistakes and write the sentences correctly.

Ex. *He hate vegetables.*
He hates vegetables.

1 You want a cup of coffee?
....

2 They not see their parents every year.
....

3 Do she have a computer at home?
....

4 He is drives to work every morning.
....

5 We start school on October.
....

6 He don't like the food in this restaurant.
....

29

6

10 ▸ **Complete the text with the Simple Present.**

My brother is great. He (Ex.) ......*plays*........ (play) baseball but he (1) .... (hate) volleyball. He (2) .... (work) very hard but he (3) .... (love) his job. He (4) .... (not clean) his house but he (5) .... (wash) his car every Saturday. He sometimes (6) .... (go) to the movies with his friends and he always (7) .... (read) the newspapers on Sunday mornings. I really (8) .... (like) my brother.

11 ▸ **Complete the sentences with the Simple Present.**

Ex. I ......*don't enjoy*............ long lectures. (not enjoy)
1 .... you .... your book every day? (read)
2 He sometimes .... football with his friends. (play)
3 They .... out very often. (not go)
4 .... she always .... you? (call)
5 He never .... running in the evening. (go)
6 .... they .... their jobs? (like)
7 I .... a lot. (not study)
8 She .... to make a mistake on the test. (not want)

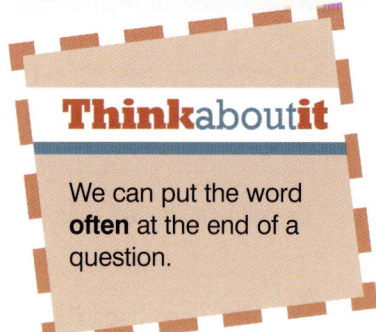

Thinkabout**it**

We can put the word **often** at the end of a question.

Pairwork

Work with a partner. Take turns. Ask and answer the following questions:

▸ Do you live in a small or large city?
▸ Do you have a car?
▸ Do you have children?
▸ What do you do on weekdays?
▸ What do you do on Saturday evening?
▸ Do you enjoy classical music?
▸ Do you play a musical instrument?
▸ Do you go to a gym?
▸ Do you play tennis?
▸ Do you watch a lot of television?

Writing

Write a paragraph about your partner using his/her answers from the questions above.

Adverbs, Too & Enough   7

Adverbs

Adjectives	Adverbs
quiet	quietly
serious	seriously
quick	quickly
bad	badly
sad	sadly
perfect	perfectly
careful	carefully
simple	simply
happy	happily
heavy	heavily
full	fully
hard	hard
fast	fast
late	late
early	early
good	well

Adverbs describe how we do something.
He works quietly.

We usually make adverbs by adding *-ly* to the adjective.
soft → softly
useful → usefully

When the adjective ends in *-y*, we take off the *-y* and add *-ily*.
heavy → heavily

When the adjective ends in *-le*, we take off the *-e* and add *-y*.
terrible → terribly

Some adverbs don't end in *-ly* and have the same form as the adjective.
hard → hard   fast → fast
early → early   late → late

Some adverbs don't end in *-ly* and have a different form from the adjective.
good → well

Adverbs that describe how we do something usually go after the main verb.
She writes clearly in her notebook.

1 Complete the sentences with adverbs.

Ex. *She drives very ...carefully... . (careful)*

1 The old man walks .... (slow)
2 Speak .... ! The baby is in bed. (quiet)
3 I speak English very .... (good)
4 Our teacher always arrives .... (late)
5 I wake up .... every morning. (early)
6 The children play .... in the playground. (noisy)
7 The boss always speaks .... to us. (polite)
8 My friend sings .... (terrible)

31

7

Too and Enough

Too has a negative meaning. It means *very much, more than is necessary or wanted*.
He can't call her. It's too early.

We sometimes use the word *too* to say that someone is too small, big, slow, etc. to do something. We use:

too + adjective/adverb + *to* + base form of verb
He's too old to go skiing.

Enough has a positive meaning. It means *as many/much as is necessary or wanted*. It goes before a noun but after an adjective or adverb.
There is enough food for dinner.
He can run a marathon. He's healthy enough.
She's on the basketball team. She plays well enough.

We often use the word *enough* to say that someone or something is small, big, slow, etc. enough to do something. We use:

enough + noun + *to* + base form of verb
He has enough gas to drive to the garage.

adjective/adverb + *enough* + *to* + base form of verb
It's warm enough to go swimming today.

2 Complete the sentences with **too** and the words in parentheses.

Ex. He's ......*too bored to work.*......
(bored, work)

1 It's .... for a walk. (hot, go)
2 The weather is .... (cold, enjoy)
3 I'm .... a car. (young, own)
4 I'm .... my parents this weekend. (busy, visit)
5 She gets home .... dinner. (late, cook)
6 This project is .... on time. (difficult, finish)

3 Choose the correct answer.

Ex. We don't have ..... for the meeting.
  a chairs enough   (b) enough chairs

1 The coffee is ..... for me. I can't drink it.
  a too sweet   b sweet enough
2 He works very ..... .
  a slow   b slowly
3 He types very ..... .
  a well   b bad
4 The guests speak ..... .
  a politely   b polite enough
5 This food is too hot ..... .
  a to eat   b eat
6 He plays tennis very ..... .
  a well   b good

4 Complete the sentences with **enough** and the words in parentheses.

Ex. The vegetables aren't ......*fresh enough to eat*...... . (fresh, eat)

1 She is .... this race. (fast, win)
2 We aren't .... to bed. (tired, go)
3 They aren't .... this car. (rich, buy)
4 I am not .... a basketball player. (tall, become)
5 It's .... today! (cold, snow)
6 That girl .... the exam. (smart, pass)

32

5 Complete the sentences with **enough** and the words in parentheses.

Ex. We don't have .... *enough time to finish* .... the project. (time, finish)

1 Does he have .... English? (experience, teach)
2 I don't have .... long books. (patience, read)
3 Do they have .... to the children? (presents, give)
4 Paul doesn't have .... his car. (money, repair)
5 Do you have .... dinner? (food, make)

6 Match.

Ex. She is fast enough to   a terribly.
1 It's too cold   b to buy for a party.
2 He cooks   c people here for the meeting.
3 There aren't enough   d noisily in this playground.
4 Children play   e to go for a walk.
5 This dress is too expensive   f on Saturday night.
6 She goes to the movies   g win the race.

Think about it

He works very hard means that he works a lot.
He works too hard means that he works more than he should.

Pairwork

Work with a partner. Take turns. Ask and answer the following questions:

- Do you go to work or school early or late?
- Do you usually come home early or late?
- Do you go to sleep early or late on Saturday night?
- Do you wake up early or late on Sunday?
- Do you play tennis well or badly?
- Do you write well or badly?
- Do you work carefully or carelessly?
- Do you speak English well or badly?

Writing

Write a paragraph about yourself with your answers to the questions above.

8 Present Continuous

Present Continuous

Affirmative
I am (I'm) working
you are (you're) working
he is (he's) working
she is (she's) working
it is (it's) working
we are (we're) working
you are (you're) working
they are (they're) working

Negative
I am not (I'm not) working
you are not (you aren't/you're not) working
he is not (he isn't/he's not) working
she is not (she isn't/she's not) working
it is not (it isn't/it's not) working
we are not (we aren't/we're not) working
you are not (you aren't/you're not) working
they are not (they aren't/they're not) working

Question
Am I working?
Are you working?
Is he working?
Is she working?
Is it working?
Are we working?
Are you working?
Are they working?

Short Answers
Yes, I am.   No, I'm not.
Yes, you are.   No, you aren't./No, you're not.
Yes, he is.   No, he isn't./No, he's not.
Yes, she is.   No, she isn't./No, she's not.
Yes, it is.   No, it isn't./No, it's not.
Yes, we are.   No, we aren't./No, we're not.
Yes, you are.   No, you aren't./No, we're not.
Yes, they are.   No, they aren't./No, they're not.

We use the Present Continuous to talk about:

➤ things that are in progress at the time of speaking.
What are they writing? They are writing an essay.

➤ things that are in progress around the time of speaking or things that are temporary.
He's applying for a new job.
She's using my office this week.

We form the Present Continuous with *am/are/is* and the base form of the verb with *-ing*.
eat   ➜   eating

When the verb ends in *-e*, we take off the *-e* and add *-ing*.
take   ➜   taking

When the verb ends in a consonant and before that consonant there is a vowel, we double the final consonant and add *-ing*.
run   ➜   running

When the verb ends in *-ie*, we take off the *-ie* and add *-y* and *-ing*.
tie   ➜   tying
lie   ➜   lying
die   ➜   dying

Notes

We can use time expressions such as *now, right now, at the moment, these days, today, this week, this month* and *this year* with the Present Continuous.
She's talking to her friend now.

34

Present Continuous 8

1 Make the -ing form of the verbs and put them in the correct part of the chart.

~~ask~~   carry   do   drive   get   have   leave   listen   make
put   shop   sleep   smile   ~~stop~~   swim   try   win   ~~write~~

run → running	take → taking	walk → walking
stopping	writing	asking

2 Complete the sentences with the Present Continuous.

Ex. He ......is writing...... an e-mail to his parents now. (write)

1 She .... to her boss. (talk)
2 Brenda .... in her armchair. (sit)
3 The girls .... Niagara Falls this week. (visit)
4 We .... golf at our club. (play)
5 My friend .... in a big race at the moment. (run)
6 Our boss .... on business this week. (travel)
7 I .... hard for my exams. (study)
8 We .... the warm weather today. (enjoy)

3 Complete the sentences with the negative form of the Present Continuous.

Ex. She ......isn't cooking...... dinner today. (cook)

1 They .... a report at the moment. (write)
2 She .... to her teacher. (listen)
3 We .... breakfast now. (eat)
4 It .... this morning. (rain)
5 I .... on the phone now. (talk)
6 Our friends .... us today. (visit)
7 Jenny .... very well at the moment. (sleep)
8 You .... the meeting. (enjoy)

Think about it

The only contraction of **I am not** is **I'm not**.

8

4 Write sentences with the Present Continuous.

Ex. *the dog / sleep / in the bedroom*
The dog isn't sleeping in the bedroom.
It is sleeping under a tree.

1 He / wash / his motorcycle
....
....

2 He / sit / on the sofa
....
....

3 the boy / look / out of the window
....
....

4 Ed and Ann / walk / in the park
....
....

5 Paul / eat / his dinner
....
....

6 the children / swim / in the sea
....
....

5 Complete the questions with the Present Continuous and write answers.

Ex. *Is Alexandra typing* a letter? (Alexandra / type) ✓
Yes, she is.

1 .... at me? (that woman / look) ✓
....

2 .... your meal? (you / enjoy) ✓
....

3 .... your new house? (workers / build) ✗
....

4 .... for a new dress? (she / shop) ✗
....

5 .... your guitar? (you / play) ✓
....

6 .... at his desk? (he / sit) ✗
....

7 .... a cake? (you / make) ✗
....

8 .... a new book? (she / buy) ✓
....

Present Continuous 8

Pairwork

Work with a partner. It is 9 o'clock on a Sunday evening. Your partner, your partner's family and a few friends are at his or her house. Ask your partner what everyone is doing.

Writing

Write an e-mail to a friend. Tell him/her:
- where you are.
- how the weather is (e.g., Is the sun shining? Is it raining/snowing?)
- what you are doing now.
- what your friends are doing.

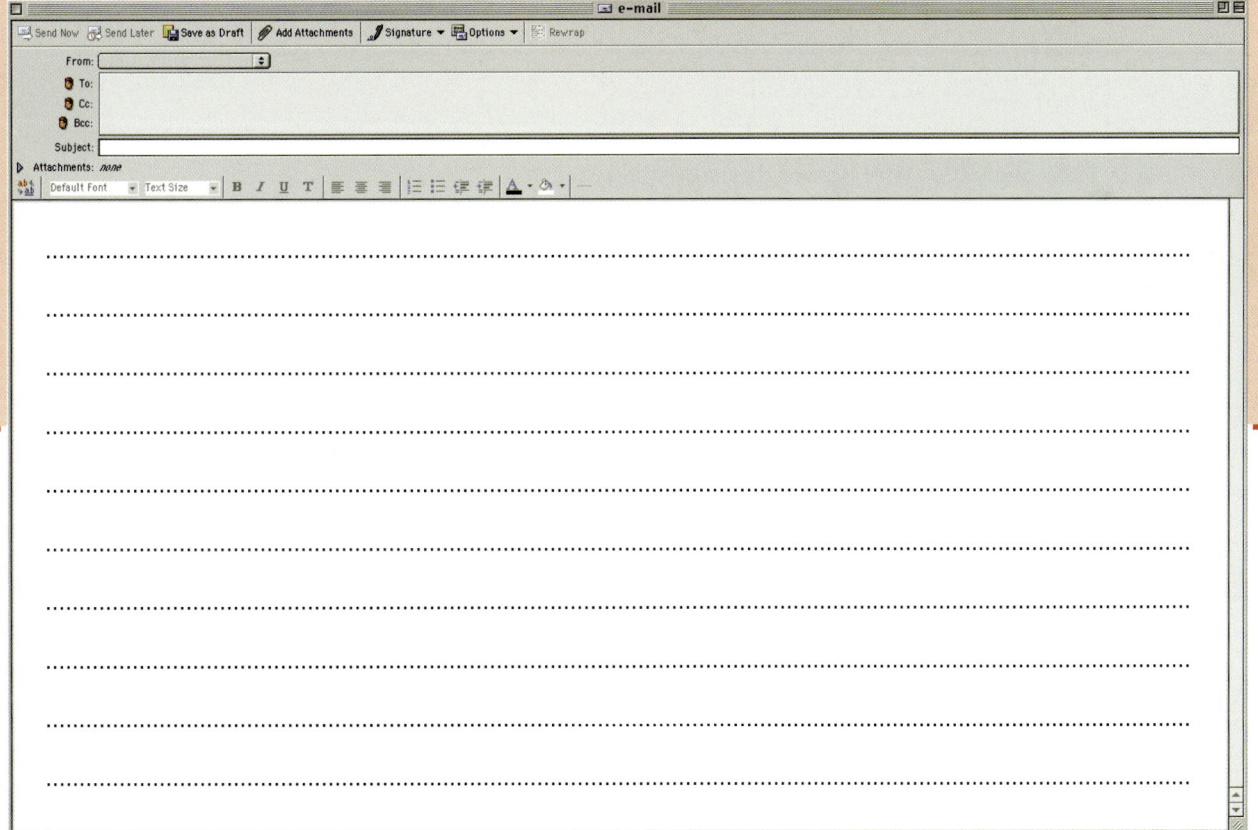

Review 2 (Units 5-8)

1 Complete the chart.

Subject Pronouns	Possessive Adjectives	Possessive Pronouns
I	my	mine
you		
he		
she		
it		–
we		
you		
they		

2 Complete the sentences with possessive adjectives.

Ex. ...*Your*... camera is in the kitchen. (you)

1 .... boss is very nice. (he)
2 .... shoes are new. (I)
3 .... car is red. (she)
4 .... brother is very tall. (he)
5 .... food is in the bowl. (it)
6 .... work is excellent. (you)
7 .... summer vacation is in July this year. (we)
8 .... restaurant is great. (they)

3 Complete the sentences with possessive pronouns.

Ex. They're your shoes. They're ......*yours*.......... .

1 It's my work. It's ....
2 It's their car. It's ....
3 It's her house. It's ....
4 They're his oranges. They're ....
5 They're her children. They're ....
6 It's your book. It's ....
7 They're his glasses. They're ....
8 They're our CDs. They're ....

38

Review 2 (Units 5-8)

4 Complete the sentences with the Simple Present.

Ex. She ......*works*........ in a bank. (work)

1. I .... spaghetti. (like)
2. William .... tennis. (not play)
3. Anna and George .... in Dallas. (not live)
4. Kate .... her car on Sundays. (wash)
5. Her brothers .... Chinese. (speak)
6. Angela .... books. (write)
7. We .... dinner at 7 o'clock. (eat)
8. They .... apple juice. (drink)

5 Complete the questions with the Simple Present and write answers.

Ex. *Do you know* .... this person? (you / know) ✓
Yes, I/we do.

1. .... English? (he / speak) ✓
....
2. .... television every evening? (they / watch) ✗
....
3. .... horses? (Janet / sometimes / ride) ✓
....
4. .... in the library? (Jason / often / study) ✓
....
5. .... at night? (he / always / cook) ✗
....
6. .... mice? (your cat / catch) ✓
....
7. .... to the movies? (you / often go) ✗
....
8. .... on Saturday? (he / sometimes / work) ✓
....

6 Choose the correct answer.

Ex. *Does she go to sleep late* in / (at) night?

1. In / At the summer we go to the beach.
2. We sometimes eat dinner on / at 6 o'clock.
3. Her exams are at / in June.
4. He goes skiing on / in the winter.
5. I always go to the movies on / at my birthday.
6. We always go to a party on / at New Year's Eve.
7. We always finish our meetings on / at 3 o'clock.
8. She swims every day at / in the evenings.

39

Review 2

7 Complete the sentences with **too** and the words in parentheses.

Ex. He is ....*too busy to call*............ you tonight. (busy, call)

1 She is .... (excited, sleep)

2 The house is .... (old, buy)

3 It's .... shopping. (rainy, go)

4 This book is .... (boring, read)

5 The project is .... (difficult, do)

6 She's .... a long way. (old, travel)

7 He's .... (young, work)

8 They're .... a mistake. (careful, make)

8 Complete the chart.

Adjectives	Adverbs
careful	*carefully*
nice	
noisy	
hard	
good	
soft	
bad	
late	
early	
perfect	
simple	
beautiful	
heavy	
slow	
gentle	
quiet	

9 Rewrite the sentences using the word given.

Ex. The orange juice is too warm to drink. (cold)
The orange juice ....*isn't cold enough*.......... to drink.

1 My work is too difficult to explain. (easy)
My work .... to explain.

2 The girl is too slow to win the race. (fast)
The girl ....
to win the race.

3 The fruit is too hard to eat. (soft)
The fruit ....
to eat.

4 This window is too dirty to see outside. (clean)
This window .... to see outside.

5 The movie is too boring to watch. (interesting)
The movie .... to watch.

6 The suitcase is too heavy to lift easily. (light)
The suitcase .... to lift easily.

40

Review 2 (Units 5-8)

10 Complete the sentences with **enough** and the words in parentheses.

Ex. There isn't ....*enough food to eat*.... at home this evening. (food, eat)

1. Katrina has .... at the moment. (things, do)
2. We don't have .... shopping. (time, go)
3. There aren't .... to everyone. (cookies, give)
4. My friend doesn't have .... his parents. (money, visit)
5. There isn't .... this evening. (time, read)
6. Do they have .... at the meeting? (coffee, drink)

11 Complete the sentences with the Present Continuous.

Ex. We ....*are studying*.... hard for our exam. (study)

1. .... it .... this morning? (snow)
2. He .... for a phone call. (wait)
3. She .... a letter at the moment. (not write)
4. They .... for a race. (practice)
5. He .... pizza now. (not eat)
6. They .... to their boss. (talk)
7. I .... at a wonderful hotel this week. (stay)
8. She .... her dog for a walk. (take)

12 Complete the questions with the Present Continuous and write answers.

Ex. *Is John washing* the car? (John / wash) ✓
    Yes, he is.

1. .... a report? (your friends / write) ✓
   ....
2. .... a pie? (she / bake) ✗
   ....
3. .... to work? (he / run) ✓
   ....
4. .... a computer game? (Emma / play) ✗
   ....
5. .... lunch for everyone? (they / buy) ✗
   ....
6. .... to the wedding? (we / go) ✗
   ....
7. .... Russian? (you / learn) ✓
   ....
8. .... soup? (you / have) ✗
   ....

9 Simple Present & Present Continuous

MEET NORMAN. HE'S WORKING AT THE MOMENT, BUT HE USUALLY DRINKS COFFEE BEHIND HIS COMPUTER.

Simple Present and Present Continuous

	Affirmative	Negative	Question
Simple Present	I work he works	I do not (don't) work he does not (doesn't) work	Do I work? Does he work?
Present Continuous	I am (I'm) working he is (he's) working you are (you're) working	I am not (I'm not) working he is not (isn't) working you are not (aren't) working	Am I working? Is he working? Are you working?

We use the Simple Present to talk about:

➤ permanent situations.
They teach math.

➤ habits.
He watches TV every evening.

➤ general truths.
Fish live in water.

We use the Present Continuous to talk about:

➤ things that are in progress at the time we are speaking.
They are sitting in the yard now.

➤ things that are in progress around the time of speaking or things that are temporary.
I am working hard today.
She is working in a bank this summer.

Time Expressions and Adverbs of Frequency

We often use adverbs of frequency (*never, sometimes, often, usually, always*) and time expressions such as *at noon, on Saturdays, every day, in the morning* and *in the summer* with the Simple Present.
They always go to work by bus.
He drinks coffee every day.

We often use time expressions such as *now, at the moment, these days, right now, these days, this year, today, tonight*, etc., with the Present Continuous.
They are reading at the moment.
She is wearing a dress today.

Simple Present & Present Continuous 9

1 Complete the sentences with the Simple Present.

Ex. They ......*don't eat*...... meat every day. (not eat)

1 She .... to work. (not walk)
2 .... they .... TV after 11 o'clock? (watch)
3 They .... by train. (always travel)
4 .... you .... chess at home? (play)
5 We .... our cousins very often. (not visit)
6 She .... breakfast at 7:30. (cook)
7 I .... a lot of history books. (read)
8 .... he .... his car every weekend? (wash)

2 Complete the sentences with the Present Continuous.

Ex. She ....*is talking*............ to her sister now. (talk)

1 He .... his black jacket today. (wear)
2 .... you .... Spanish? (learn)
3 They .... with their parents. (live)
4 We .... the bedroom now. (not paint)
5 Their children .... their bikes at the moment. (ride)
6 .... she .... to her aunt? (write)
7 I .... science at the moment. (not study)
8 She .... to the radio. (listen)

3 Put the words and expressions in the correct column.

at the moment   right now   usually   now   never   this year
always   today   every day   on Mondays   this month   sometimes

Simple Present	Present Continuous
never	*at the moment*

43

10 Can & Must

NO, NORMAN. YOU CAN'T CATCH A COMPUTER VIRUS.

Can

Affirmative	Negative	Question
I can run	I cannot (can't) run	Can I run?
you can run	you cannot (can't) run	Can you run?
he can run	he cannot (can't) run	Can he run?
she can run	she cannot (can't) run	Can she run?
it can run	it cannot (can't) run	Can it run?
we can run	we cannot (can't) run	Can we run?
you can run	you cannot (can't) run	Can you run?
they can run	they cannot (can't) run	Can they run?

Short Answers

Yes, I can.	No, I can't.
Yes, you can.	No, you can't.
Yes, he can.	No, he can't.
Yes, she can.	No, she can't.
Yes, it can.	No, it can't.
Yes, we can.	No, we can't.
Yes, you can.	No, you can't.
Yes, they can.	No, they can't.

We use *can* to talk about ability. *Can* is followed by the base form of the verb.
I can play the guitar.
Can she drive a car?
They can't speak French.

We also use *can* to ask for or give permission to do something.
Can I use your computer today?
He can borrow my car tomorrow.

We use *can* to talk about the present and the future.
I can leave the office now.
They can relax on Saturday.

We often use *can* with verbs of sense, such as *see, hear, smell,* etc.
Can you hear music?
I can smell smoke!

1 Complete the sentences with **can** and the verbs in parentheses.

Ex. I ...*can swim*... really fast. (swim)

1 .... he .... tennis? (play)
2 We .... to the movies today. (not go)
3 She .... that report for me. (write)
4 I .... his name. (not remember)
5 .... we .... your boat for the day? (borrow)
6 They .... the piano. (not play)
7 He .... his watch. (not find)
8 .... you .... to the beach from here? (walk)

2 Complete the sentences with **can** and the verbs in parentheses.

Ex. ...Can... we ...order... a pizza for lunch? (order)

1 You .... out today! It's my birthday! (not go)
2 It's cold! .... you .... the door? (close)
3 We .... your parents on Sunday. (visit)
4 .... we .... our friends tomorrow? (see)
5 .... I .... in the yard next week? (work)
6 They .... to music now. It's very late! (not listen)
7 .... you .... that report for me? (type)
8 I .... now. I have an important meeting in five minutes. (not talk)

3 Write questions and answers.

Ex. *he / run fast / ?* ✓
Can he run fast?
Yes, he can.

1 I / cook our dinner / ? ✓
....
....

2 they / fix the computer / ? ✗
....
....

3 she / carry the package / ? ✓
....
....

4 you / buy me a ticket / ? ✓
....
....

5 I / bake a cake / ? ✓
....
....

6 they / do that project / ? ✓
....
....

7 she / learn English / ? ✓
....
....

8 you / wash the car / ? ✗
....
....

Must

Affirmative
I must go
you must go
he must go
she must go
it must go
we must go
you must go
they must go

Negative
I must not go
you must not go
he must not go
she must not go
it must not go
we must not go
you must not go
they must not go

We use *must* to talk about obligation, rules and laws. *Must* is followed by the base form of the verb.
I must go to the doctor.
You must invite them to dinner next week.

We use *must not* to talk about things we are not allowed to do (prohibition). *Must not* is also followed by a base form.
You must not go in there.
You must not take things without asking.

We use *must* to talk about the present and the future.
You must speak to him now.
They must finish their project next month.

Notes

The form *mustn't* and questions with *must* are not common in American English.

It is not very polite to use *must* when we are talking to someone we don't know well or to someone who is older than us.

47

10

4 **Complete the sentences with must or must not.**

Ex. You *must not* smoke in the office. ✗

1 You .... use your camera in this art gallery. ✗

2 You .... wait at the red traffic light. ✓

3 You .... watch TV all day. ✗

4 You .... wear a seat belt in your car. ✓

5 You .... make a lot of noise in the hospital. ✗

6 You .... recycle paper. ✓

7 You .... leave your dog in a car in the summer. ✗

8 You .... pass a test to get a driver's license. ✓

Think about it

We never put **to** after **must**.

5 **Write sentences with must or must not.**

Ex. you / go to work / every day ✓
You must go to work every day.

1 we / talk in the library ✗
....

2 I / do my math homework / now ✓
....

3 we / write the report / on Sunday ✓
....

4 they / write on the walls ✗
....

5 she / remember her appointment ✓
....

6 I / forget my glasses ✗
....

7 I / be late for the meeting ✗
....

8 we / be rude to our guests. ✗
....

48

6 Write rules for the office with must and must not. Use the phrases in the box.

OFFICE RULES

MUST

Ex.	You must come to work on time.
1	
2	
3	
4	

MUST NOT

5	
6	
7	
8	

- be late for meetings
- ~~come to work on time~~
- answer e-mails quickly
- eat or drink near your computer
- be polite to customers
- make personal phone calls
- leave the coffee room clean
- turn off your computer at night
- leave before 5:00 p.m.

Pairwork

Work with a partner. Ask and answer questions with *can*.

- ➤ send an e-mail
- ➤ drive a car
- ➤ ride a horse
- ➤ speak Spanish
- ➤ swim a long way
- ➤ write songs

Writing

Write a paragraph about your family. Describe:

- ➤ what each person can/can't do.
- ➤ what each person must/must not do.

49

11 Imperative, Let's & Object Pronouns

Imperative

We use the imperative when:

➤ we give instructions.
Open your books to page 15.

➤ we want to prevent something bad from happening.
Don't walk on the ice. It's dangerous!

We form the imperative with the base form of the verb. We use it with an exclamation point (!) to show strong emotion. The form is the same when we speak to one person or to several people.
Pick that bag up, Brian!   Wait here, children!

We form the negative imperative with the word *don't*.
Don't push!   Don't stay out in the rain!

We often use the word *please* with an imperative. It sounds more polite.
Please turn off the radio.   Open the window, please.

1 Complete the sentences with the imperative or negative imperative of the words in the box.

drink   eat   help   listen   miss   read   shout   sit   ~~turn~~

Ex. ......*Turn*...... off the light, please. ✓

1 .... lots of water in hot weather. ✓
2 .... at me! I can hear you. ✗
3 .... to this music. It's great. ✓
4 .... your carrots. They're good for you. ✓
5 .... near the fire. It's hot! ✗
6 .... this, please. It's important. ✓
7 .... me! This box is very heavy. ✓
8 .... the Grand Canyon when you go to the USA! ✗

Imperative, Let's & Object Pronouns 11

Let's

We use *Let's* with the base form of the verb for suggestions.
Let's play tennis!
Let's go for a walk.

We form the negative with the word *not*. *Not* goes between *Let's* and the base form.
Let's not stay home this evening.
Let's not get up early tomorrow.

2 Complete the sentences with let's or let's not and the words in the box.

~~buy~~	have	meet	park	wait
	watch	write		

Ex. *Let's buy* a magazine. ✓

1 .... a cup of coffee. ✓
2 .... a letter. We can send an e-mail. ✗
3 .... for your cousin outside. It's cold. ✗
4 .... here. We can walk to the station. ✓
5 .... at the bus stop. ✓
6 .... TV. It's a nice day. ✗

3 Complete the sentences with the words in the box.

~~be~~	cook	~~go~~	listen	make
take	talk	touch	visit	wake

Ex. "Let's ..... *go* ..... for a walk in the park."
"OK, but don't ..... *be* ..... late for dinner."

1 "Let's .... lunch now."
"OK, but don't .... a mess."
2 "Let's .... to some music."
"OK, but don't .... the baby."
3 "Let's .... your cousin."
"OK, but don't .... about football."
4 "Let's .... a look at your brother's new computer."
"OK, but don't .... it!"

Object Pronouns

Subject Pronouns	Object Pronouns
I	me
you	you
he	him
she	her
it	it
we	us
you	you
they	them

We use object pronouns to replace an object in a sentence.
He is holding **a pen**. → He is holding **it**.
I can see **your son**. → I can see **him**.

4 Complete the sentences with object pronouns.

Ex. I can't find ..... *them* ..... . (the photos)

1 They visit .... every weekend. (we)
2 Whose is .... ? (the pencil)
3 I don't know .... (that boy)
4 They work with .... (my sister)
5 She has a gift for .... (I)
6 He can't swim! Help .... ! (he)
7 Can you hear .... ? (the bell)
8 Don't break .... (the cups)
9 I see .... every day. (my aunt)
10 He doesn't like .... (we)

51

11

5 Rewrite the sentences using the imperative.

Ex. *You must stay here.*
Stay here.

1 You must be careful with the piano.
....
2 You must not drink all the lemonade.
....
3 You must not make noise.
....
4 You must not read that letter.
....
5 You must call him now.
....

6 Find the mistakes and write the sentences correctly.

Ex. *Don't to open the window.*
Don't open the window.

1 Let's to go to the park.
....
2 Where's the newspaper? Please help me find her.
....
3 Don't to tell her the news.
....
4 Let's not to stay here. It's not nice.
....
5 They can't visit we.
....

7 Rewrite the sentences. Change the underlined words to object pronouns.

Ex. *Take the letters to your boss.*
Take them to your boss.

1 Let's buy the bread from the bakery.
....
2 You can invite your friend and his cousin.
....
3 He doesn't talk to my brother and me every day.
....
4 Please don't give the pens to your sister.
....
5 We don't like very hot weather.
....
6 Send the e-mail to your brother now, please.
....

Think about it

We can put the word **please** at the beginning or at the end of a sentence.

Pairwork

Work with a partner. Take turns. Make suggestions and comments like the examples in exercise 3.

Writing

You are going on vacation with a friend. Write four suggestions with *Let's* and four with *Let's not*.

Simple Past: To Be   12

THERE WEREN'T ENOUGH CHAIRS IN THE MEETING ROOM.

NORMAN, PLEASE FIND ANOTHER CHAIR!

Simple Past: To Be

Affirmative	Negative	Question
I was	I was not (wasn't)	Was I?
you were	you were not (weren't)	Were you?
he was	he was not (wasn't)	Was he?
she was	she was not (wasn't)	Was she?
it was	it was not (wasn't)	Was it?
we were	we were not (weren't)	Were we?
you were	you were not (weren't)	Were you?
they were	they were not (weren't)	Were they?

Short Answers

Yes, I was.	No, I wasn't.
Yes, you were.	No, you weren't.
Yes, he was.	No, he wasn't.
Yes, she was.	No, she wasn't.
Yes, it was.	No, it wasn't.
Yes, we were.	No, we weren't.
Yes, you were.	No, you weren't.
Yes, they were.	No, they weren't.

The Simple Past of the verb *to be* is *was/were*.
My book was on this table yesterday.
They were on vacation last week.

We form the negative by putting the word *not* after the verb. The short form is *wasn't/weren't*.
She was not happy.
They weren't in the office last Monday.

We form the question by changing the word order of the subject and the verb.
Were they on vacation last week?

Notes

We use time expressions such as *yesterday, yesterday morning, last Saturday* and *last week* with the Simple Past. These expressions can start or end a sentence.

---

1 Complete the sentences with **was** or **were**.

Ex. They ......*were*...... at work yesterday afternoon.

1 The boss ...*was*...... very angry yesterday.
2 They ...*were*...... in Dallas last month.
3 I ......*was*........ busy yesterday morning.
4 My brother and I ...*were*...... sick last week.
5 Tanya and Sonya ...*were*...... at home last night.
6 She ...*was*...... in high school two years ago.
7 We ...*were*...... happy to see you last Monday.
8 You ...*were*...... in the office early this morning.

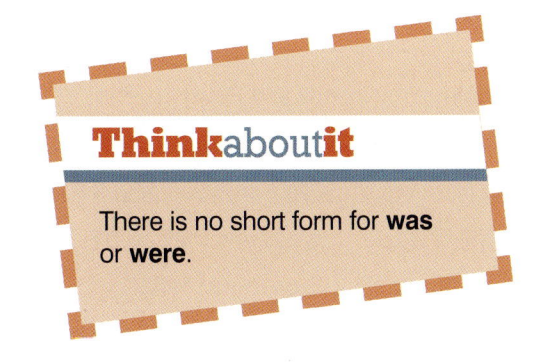

Think about it

There is no short form for **was** or **were**.

53

12

2 Make the sentences negative.

Ex. *He was at a meeting yesterday.*
He wasn't at a meeting yesterday.

1 They were at the concert last night.
....
2 It was an exciting movie.
....
3 She was frightened on the plane.
....
4 You were good at math in high school.
....
5 He was with the boss at lunchtime.
....
6 I was at the mall yesterday afternoon.
....

3 Complete the questions with **was** or **were** and write answers.

Ex. *Was* the painting on this wall? ✓
Yes, it was.

1 .... they in the park yesterday? ✗
....
2 .... you pleased with the present? ✓
....
3 .... she on television last night? ✗
....
4 .... your sunglasses in the car on Saturday? ✓
....
5 .... you a good student in high school? ✓
....
6 .... the music very bad? ✗
....

4 Write questions and answers.

Ex. *your glasses / on your desk / ? (on the kitchen table)*
Were your glasses on your desk?
No, they weren't. They were on the kitchen table.

1 his hat / black / ? (brown)
....
....
2 Paul and Tom / at the theater / last night / ? (last Friday)
....
....
3 the flowers / yellow / ? (pink)
....
....
4 the pizzas / at the restaurant / expensive / ? (very cheap)
....
....
5 the young boy / hungry / ? (thirsty)
....
....

5 Complete the text with **was, wasn't, were** or **weren't**.

Last summer my friends and I (Ex.) ....*were*.... on vacation in New York City. Our hotel (1) .... beautiful and close to Central Park. The hotel employees (2) .... friendly and helpful. The city (3) .... exciting. The streets (4) .... very crowded, and the noise from the traffic (5) .... unbelievable! The museums and parks (6) .... great, and the zoo (7) .... a lot of fun, too! The restaurants (8) .... cheap, but the food (9) .... delicious! I (10) .... bored for a minute, and my friends and I (11) .... all very busy with our cameras. It (12) .... a great vacation!

Simple Past: To Be 12

There Was / There Were

Affirmative	Negative	Question
there was	there was not (there wasn't)	Was there?
there were	there were not (there weren't)	Were there?

We use *there was* and *there were* to talk or ask about what existed in the past.
There was a big dog in the garden.
There were only three people at the meeting.
Were there apples on the tree?

Short Answers

Yes, there was.   No, there wasn't.
Yes, there were.   No, there weren't.

6 Complete the sentences with the correct form of *there was*/*were*.

Ex. ....*There were*.... many people in the park. ✓
1 .... many stores in the town. ✗
2 .... anything on the desk. ✗
3 .... three men in the boat. ✓
4 .... some flowers in the vase. ✓
5 .... a television in the room. ✗
6 .... a notebook on the desk?
7 .... a swimming pool at the hotel. ✓
8 .... many fish in the river?

Pairwork

Work with a partner. Take turns. Ask and answer the following questions:
- Where was your last vacation?
- Were you in a big or small city?
- Were you in a foreign country?
- Were you near the sea?
- Was it a quiet place or a noisy place?
- Were you with friends or family?
- Was it boring or exciting?
- Was the weather hot?

Writing

Write a paragraph about your last vacation. Use the questions above to help you.

Review 3 (Units 9-12)

1 Complete the sentences with the Simple Present.

Ex. He ....*reads*......... a newspaper every day. (read)

1. Tigers .... in jungles. (live)
2. .... he .... in the city? (work)
3. .... they .... on vacation every summer? (go)
4. The doctor .... in at 9:15. (come)
5. She .... sad movies. (not like)
6. We .... your story. (not believe)
7. He .... the birds every morning. (feed)
8. They .... tennis in the rain. (not play)

2 Complete the sentences with the Present Continuous.

Ex. He ....*is getting*......... ready to go out. (get)

1. They .... their house at the moment. (paint)
2. Don't go out! It .... dark now. (get)
3. The students .... hard this year. (study)
4. .... Gerald .... the money? (count)
5. She .... the housework this morning. (not do)
6. .... you .... to work today? (walk)
7. They .... for a new house. (not look)
8. I .... to the gym now. (go)

3 Complete the sentences with the Simple Present or Present Continuous.

Ex. They ....*are looking*......... at my vacation photos now. (look)

1. They .... a meeting at the moment. (not have)
2. He always .... me in the morning. (call)
3. Look! He .... a photo of you. (take)
4. I .... a lot of money. (not spend)
5. Emma and Greta .... chess every Saturday. (play)
6. .... it .... here every winter? (snow)
7. He .... to us very often. (not speak)
8. .... they .... for the bus now? (wait)

56

Review 3 (Units 9-12)

4 ▸ Complete the sentences with **can** and the verbs in parentheses.

Ex. They ......*can't understand*.... this letter. *(not understand)*

1. He .... very well. (swim)
2. We .... Peter to come. He isn't home now. (not ask)
3. .... you .... Chinese food? (cook)
4. I .... these questions. (not answer)
5. She .... the work now. She's too tired. (not do)
6. They .... the telephone number. (not remember)
7. .... he .... computers? (fix)
8. My glasses were here but I .... them now. (not find)

5 ▸ Write questions with **can** and write answers.

Ex. they / come / to the office / on Saturday / ? ✗
Can they come to the office on Saturday?
No, they can't.

1. you / understand / Japanese / ? ✓
   ....
   ....

2. He / play a musical instrument / ? ✗
   ....
   ....

3. I / borrow / your watch / ? ✗
   ....
   ....

4. we / go / for lunch / ? ✓
   ....
   ....

5. they / bring / the CDs this afternoon / ? ✓
   ....
   ....

6. I / have / the newspaper / ? ✓
   ....
   ....

7. you / clean / the windows / today / ? ✗
   ....
   ....

8. you / remember / her name / ? ✗
   ....
   ....

6 ▸ Complete the sentences with **must** and the verbs in parentheses.

Ex. Passengers ....*must show*.......... their tickets at the gate. (show)

1. You .... your cell phone in the library. (turn off)
2. They .... a uniform at work. (wear)
3. We .... him in the hospital. (visit)
4. You .... the front door open. (not leave)
5. You .... the report. (finish)
6. You .... trash on the street. (not throw)
7. You .... your computer with water. (not clean)
8. We .... the car to the mechanic. (take)

57

13 Simple Past Affirmative: Regular & Irregular Verbs

HE CLEANED HIS OFFICE TWO YEARS AGO. THEN HE WENT ON A CLEANING STRIKE.

Simple Past Affirmative

Regular Verbs
I walked
you walked
he walked
she walked
it walked
we walked
you walked
they walked

Irregular Verbs
I went
you went
he went
she went
it went
we went
you went
they went

We use the Simple Past to talk about:

➤ actions that started and ended in the past.
I walked to work yesterday.

➤ actions in the past that were habits.
When he was young, he went out every weekend.

➤ a series of actions in the past.
He got into the car, opened the window and drove away.

We form the Simple Past of most regular verbs by adding *-ed* to the base form of the verb.
walk ➡ walked

When the verb ends in *-e*, we add *-d*.
live ➡ lived

When the verb ends in a consonant and *-y*, we take off the *-y* and add *-ied*.
carry ➡ carried

When the verb ends in a vowel and *-y*, we just add *-ed*.
play ➡ played

When the verb ends in a vowel and a consonant and the last syllable is stressed, we double the last consonant and add *-ed*.
permit ➡ permitted

There are many irregular verbs in English. We do not form the Simple Past of these verbs by adding *-ed*. See the Irregular Verbs list on page 98.

13 Simple Past Affirmative: Regular & Irregular Verbs

1 Complete the sentences with the Simple Past.

Ex. We ....*played*.... football yesterday. (play)

1. They ....cleaned.... the kitchen on Tuesday. (clean)
2. He ....reached.... the office at 9 o'clock. (reach)
3. She ....asked.... me a lot of questions. (ask)
4. I ....scored.... ten points in the basketball game yesterday. (score)
5. You ....pushed.... me! (push)
6. He ....opened.... the door for me. (open)
7. We ....listened.... to his new CD yesterday. (listen)
8. They ....moved.... the desk into the other room. (move)

Think about it

We do not double the **n** in **open** or **listen** because we stress the first syllable.

2 Complete the charts.

Verb	Simple Past
begin	*began*
break	broke
buy	bought
come	came
do	did
eat	ate
find	found
get	got

Verb	Simple Past
give	gave
have	had
know	knew
leave	left
make	made
see	saw
take	too
write	wrote

3 Complete the sentences with the Simple Past.

Ex. They ....*came*.... to work at 10 o'clock. (come)

1. He ....bought.... some magazines yesterday. (buy)
2. There is no cake. They ....ate.... it all this morning. (eat)
3. I ....saw.... him two days ago. He was fine. (see)
4. I ....did.... all my work quickly. (do)
5. We ....had.... chicken sandwiches for lunch. (have)
6. She ....found.... her keys under the sofa. (find)
7. I ....gave.... him the report before lunch.
8. He ....left.... his watch on the dining room table. (leave)

4 Complete the sentences with the Simple Past. Use the words in the box.

| begin | borrow | break | carry | help | make | stay | study | take |

Ex. They ....*began*.... work early yesterday.

1. He ....broke.... two plates last night.
2. They ....carried.... the furniture up the stairs.
3. We ....took.... photos at the zoo.
4. He ....made.... lunch on Wednesday.
5. She ....stayed.... with the children all morning.
6. They ....helped.... me with my homework.
7. I ....studied.... hard for the final exam.
8. My brother ....borrowed.... my car yesterday.

61

13

Ago

We use the word *ago* with a period of time (e.g., minutes, days, years) to describe actions that happened at a specific time in the past.
She finished high school a year ago.
I saw her in her office twenty minutes ago.
He got a new job two months ago.

5 Write sentences with ago.

Ex. He arrived at 9 o'clock. It is now 11 o'clock.
He arrived two hours ago.

1 I called her on Tuesday. It is now Friday.
....

2 He bought a new car in July. It is now November.
....

3 They went to the library at 6:30. It's 7:30 now.
....

4 I painted this picture when I was 24. I am now 30.
....

Think about it

We say **three years ago**, not **before three years**.

5 They spoke to him on Saturday. It is now Monday.
....

6 I gave him that book when he was 10. He is now 16.
....

6 Write the words in the correct order.

Ex. a / sofa / new / bought / yesterday / they
They bought a new sofa yesterday.

1 night / to / theater / I / the / last / went
....

2 ago / he / me / gave / pen / this / a / week
....

3 Saturday / we / a / lot / money / of / spent / on
....

4 last / she / her / sister / week / visited
....

5 computer / afternoon / they / the / yesterday / fixed
....

7 Find the mistakes and write the sentences correctly.

Ex. They yesterday listened to my new CD.
They listened to my new CD yesterday.

1 She wake up at 6 o'clock this morning.
....

2 I take this photo two days ago.
....

3 They studies English in Chicago last year.
....

4 We flew to Brazil before two months.
....

5 He tells me the answer last night.
....

Simple Past Affirmative: Regular & Irregular Verbs 13

8 Complete the text with the Simple Past.

A new Chinese restaurant (Ex.) ...*opened*... (open) in town last week and we (1) .... (decide) to go there on Saturday. We (2) .... (go) there early and we (3) .... (get) a table easily. There (4) .... (be) Chinese decorations on all the walls and they (5) .... (play) Chinese music all evening. The waiters (6) .... (wear) Chinese clothes so it (7) .... (feel) like we (8) .... (be) in China! We all (9) .... (order) different things and we (10) .... (share) our food.

At the end of the meal, our waiter (11) .... (bring) us the check. Because the service and food (12) .... (be) good, we (13) .... (leave) a tip when we (14) .... (pay). I think this restaurant is the best in town.

Pairwork

Work with a partner. Talk about what you did last Saturday. Start like this:
On Saturday morning I ... .

Writing

You are on vacation. Write a postcard to a friend. Describe your first day. Tell him/her:

- what time you arrived
- what you did first
- what you did after that
- what you saw
- what you ate
- who you met

63

14 Simple Past Negative & Question

DID SOMEBODY TURN OFF THE HEAT?

Simple Past Negative and Question

Affirmative	Negative	Question
I worked	I did not (didn't) work	Did I work?
you worked	you did not (didn't) work	Did you work?
he worked	he did not (didn't) work	Did he work?
she worked	she did not (didn't) work	Did she work?
it worked	it did not (didn't) work	Did it work?
we worked	we did not (didn't) work	Did we work?
you worked	you did not (didn't) work	Did you work?
they worked	they did not (didn't) work	Did they work?

Short Answers

Yes, I did.	No, I didn't.
Yes, you did.	No, you didn't.
Yes, he did.	No, he didn't.
Yes, she did.	No, she didn't.
Yes, it did.	No, it didn't.
Yes, we did.	No, we didn't.
Yes, you did.	No, you didn't.
Yes, they did.	No, they didn't.

We form the negative of the Simple Past (regular and irregular verbs) with the auxiliary verb *did*, the word *not* and the base form of the verb.
He didn't like the book.
I didn't write that letter.

We form the question of the Simple Past (regular and irregular verbs) with *did* and the base form of the verb.
Did he like the movie?
Did you write that letter?

1 Complete the sentences with the negative form of the Simple Past.

Ex. They .... *didn't stay* .... out all day. (stay)

1. Alice .... the orange juice. (drink)
2. We .... the music very loud. (play)
3. I .... ice cream for dessert. (want)
4. He .... me the news. (tell)
5. She .... the boss yesterday. (see)
6. He .... the dishes yesterday. (do)
7. They .... on the computer last week. (work)
8. I .... your cup. (break)

Simple Past Negative & Question **14**

2 Complete the questions with the Simple Past.

Ex. *Did you brush* your teeth this morning? (you / brush)
1 .... all the work last night? (they / finish)
2 .... that picture? (she / draw)
3 .... to Maria two days ago? (you / speak)
4 .... to work on time? (they / get)
5 .... to the bank yesterday? (he / go)
6 .... John to dinner? (Paula / invite)
7 .... last night? (it / rain)
8 .... television yesterday evening? (you / watch)

3 Make the sentences negative.

Ex. *I took your pen.*
I didn't take your pen.

1 He fell down the stairs yesterday.
....
2 I forgot the bananas.
....
3 We chose our new carpet this morning.
....
4 They stayed in the house all day yesterday.
....
5 She read the book in two days.
....
6 He did well in high school.
....

Think about it

Be careful with the verb **do**:

Affirmative: I **did** my homework.
Negative: I **didn't do** my homework.
Question: **Did** you **do** your homework?

4 Write questions.

Ex. *He stood on the chair.*
Did he stand on the chair?

1 They knew the way to the mall.
....
2 He thought it was funny.
....
3 They studied in Japan.
....
4 He bought presents for the children.
....
5 They won the game easily.
....
6 He drove to the airport.
....
7 The train stopped suddenly.
....
8 The children hated the old house.
....

5 Write the words in the correct order.

Ex. *she / this / did / leave / morning / ?*
Did she leave this morning?

1 have / for / we / lunch / didn't / spaghetti.
....
2 sleep / eight / last / I / for / night / didn't / hours
....
3 lake / did / swim / you / in / the / ?
....
4 take / she / her / didn't / coat
....
5 the / did / pay / you / phone bill / yesterday / ?
....
6 he / finger / did / his / cut / ?
....

65

14

6 ▸ Write questions for the answers.

Ex. *Did he run to the bank?*
Yes, he ran to the bank.

1 ....
No, they didn't play basketball.

2 ....
Yes, she taught physics.

3 ....
Yes, she had eggs for breakfast.

4 ....
No, the movie didn't start at 6 o'clock.

5 ....
Yes, we drove to the lake.

6 ....
Yes, Mr. Peterson sold his store.

7 ....
No, I didn't drink coffee this morning.

8 ....
No, we didn't enjoy the vacation.

Pairwork

Work with a partner. Take turns. Ask and answer the following questions about last Saturday:

- ▸ Did you get up early on Saturday morning?
- ▸ Did you have coffee with your breakfast?
- ▸ Did you read a newspaper?
- ▸ Did you meet a friend in the morning?
- ▸ Did you have lunch at home?
- ▸ Did you go shopping?
- ▸ Did you go out in the evening?
- ▸ Did you watch a movie on TV?
- ▸ Did you have a relaxing day?
- ▸ Did you feel tired at the end of the day?

Writing

Write eight things you didn't do last weekend.

Some, Any, No, Every   15

I'M SURE THE REPORT IS SOMEWHERE ON MY DESK.

Some, Any, No

We use the word *some* before a noun in an affirmative sentence to say that something exists.
There is some money in my bag.
There are some sandwiches on the plate.

We use the word *any* in negative sentences and questions to say that something doesn't exist or to ask if something exists.
There aren't any glasses on the table.
Are there any apples on the tree?

We can use the word *no* plus a noun after an affirmative verb to make a sentence negative in meaning.
There are no books in the cupboard. (There aren't any books in the cupboard.)

Notes

We can use the word *some* in questions with *can* to ask for something or to offer something.
Can I have some water, please?
Can I get you some fruit from the market?

---

1 **Complete the sentences with some or any.**

Ex. We don't have ...*any*... envelopes.

1. Are there .... cups in the sink?
2. There are .... nice jackets in that store.
3. Can I give you .... more soup?
4. We don't have .... cookies or milk.
5. They don't want .... help.
6. Can I have .... cheese on my sandwich, please?
7. He doesn't have .... art books.
8. There is .... milk in the refrigerator.

67

2 Complete the sentences with any or no.

Ex. There is ......*no*...... butter on my sandwich.

1. We didn't take .... warm clothes.
2. They had .... chocolate cake.
3. He doesn't have .... shampoo.
4. There is .... work for you today.
5. There was .... salt in the soup.
6. I don't have .... batteries for the radio.
7. She took .... photos at the wedding.
8. He didn't drink .... water.

Someone, Anyone, No One, Everyone

People	Things	Places
someone/somebody	something	somewhere
anyone/anybody	anything	anywhere
no one/nobody	nothing	nowhere
everyone/everybody	everything	everywhere

We usually use the words that begin with *some-* in affirmative sentences.

We use the words *someone* and *somebody* to talk about one unspecified person. There is no difference between *someone* and *somebody*.
Someone put your umbrella outside. = Somebody put your umbrella outside.

We use the word *something* to talk about one unspecified thing.
There was something in my cup of tea.

We use the word *somewhere* to talk about one unspecified place.
Can we go somewhere quiet?

We use the words *anyone/anybody*, *anything* and *anywhere* to talk about one unspecified person, thing or place. We usually use the words that begin with *any-* in negative sentences and questions.
There isn't anybody in the room. = There isn't anyone in the room.
Do you want anything for dessert?
I can't find the cat anywhere.

We use the words *no one/nobody*, *nothing* and *nowhere* in affirmative sentences when the verb is affirmative but the meaning of the sentence is negative.
No one saw the boss yesterday. = Nobody saw the boss yesterday.
Nothing happened at the office.
Your notebook is nowhere on my desk.

We use the words *everyone/everybody*, *everything* and *everywhere* to talk about all the people, things or places. When *everyone/everybody* or *everything* is the subject of a sentence, it is followed by a verb in the third person singular.
Everyone watches that show on TV. = Everybody watches that show on TV.
Everything was perfect at the hotel.
I looked everywhere for my keys, but I didn't find them.

3 Complete the sentences with someone, anyone or everyone.

Ex. There's ......*someone*.......... at the front door.

1. I didn't know .... at the meeting yesterday.
2. .... took my pen last night.
3. I don't think .... can answer this question. It's very difficult.
4. .... knows the words to that song.
5. There must be .... at home. The lights are on.
6. Don't tell .... my secret.

Think about it

We can use **some** and words that begin with **some-** in questions to offer something to someone or to ask for something.
Do you want something to drink?

4 Rewrite each sentence with the word given. Use between two and five words in the blank.

Ex. *There isn't anything in your hand. (nothing)*
There ....*is nothing*........ in your hand.

1 There are no new books in the library. (any)
   There .... in the library.
2 There isn't anybody at home. (nobody)
   There .... at home.
3 They had no money in the bank. (any)
   They .... money in the bank.
4 He took nothing with him. (anything)
   He .... with him.
5 My keys are nowhere in the house. (anywhere)
   My keys .... in the house.

Think about it

We cannot use **everyone** or **everybody** after **There is**.

5 Choose the correct answer.

Ex. Can you give me .... to eat?
    a nothing   b everything   **(c) something**

1 Did you look .... for your watch?
   a anywhere   b everywhere   c somewhere
2 Not .... wants to go; only three or four of us.
   a anyone   b someone   c everyone
3 There was .... in your office five minutes ago.
   a somebody   b anybody   c everybody
4 I didn't have .... for breakfast.
   a nothing   b something   c anything
5 There isn't .... I can do. I'm sorry.
   a anything   b nothing   c something
6 I don't remember .... about it.
   a nothing   b anything   c something

Pairwork

Work with a partner. Take turns. Ask and answer questions about the room or building you are in. Use language from this unit.

Writing

Write a paragraph about your home and the things in it. Use *some, any, no, every,* and other language in this unit.

16 Count & Noncount Nouns & Quantifiers

YOUR GOAL FOR NEXT YEAR IS TO DO SOME WORK.

Count and Noncount Nouns

Count Nouns
cat
desk
fork
photo
picture
stamp
train
umbrella
watch
woman

Noncount Nouns
bread
butter
cheese
furniture
ice
meat
milk
money
news
rice
water

Nouns that we can count and that we can use in the plural are called count nouns. When the subject of a sentence is a plural count noun, we use a verb in the third person plural.
There were three photos on the desk.
Three men work in the office.

Nouns that we cannot count and that do not have plurals are noncount nouns. We do not use *a* and *an* with noncount nouns. When the subject of a sentence is a noncount noun, we use a verb in the third person singular.
Our furniture is quite old.
Your money is on the table.

We can use certain quantity phrases before noncount nouns to make them countable: e.g., *a glass of* (water), *a slice of* (bread), *a piece of* (cheese), *a carton of* (milk), *a bag/bowl of rice, a pound/kilo of* (sugar, beef, etc.).

We can use the word *some* in front of count and noncount nouns in affirmative sentences.
There are some stamps in her bag.
There is some ice in my juice.

We can use the word *any* in front of count and noncount nouns in negative sentences and questions.
There isn't any milk left.
Are there any mirrors in the room?

We can use the word *no* in front of count and noncount nouns with an affirmative verb to give a sentence a negative meaning.
There are no pictures on the wall.
There is no bread in the kitchen.

1 Choose the correct answer.

Ex. *There* is / (are) *some flowers on the table.*

1 *Is / Are* there any ice in the drinks?
2 The cheese *is / are* delicious.
3 *Is / Are* the money in the envelopes?
4 There *is / are* some nice plates on the table.
5 There *is / are* two slices of bread on the plate.
6 There *is / are* some cold water in the glass.
7 The news *was / were* good.
8 Furniture *costs / cost* a lot of money.

70

Count & Noncount Nouns & Quantifiers **16**

2 Complete the sentences with **a, an** or **some**.

Ex. There were ...*some*... toys on the floor.

1. There's .... envelope here with no name on it.
2. There were .... olives on the pizza.
3. We need .... more cheese for the sandwiches.
4. I saw .... insect in the shower.
5. She is .... famous singer.
6. There are .... pears on the kitchen table.
7. I always have .... cup of coffee in the morning.
8. I put .... butter on my toast.

Thinkaboutit

We do not use **a** or **an** with noncount nouns.

3 Match and make phrases. Then write the phrases under the pictures.

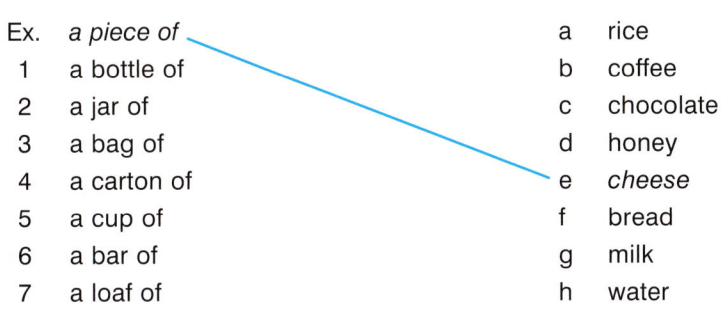

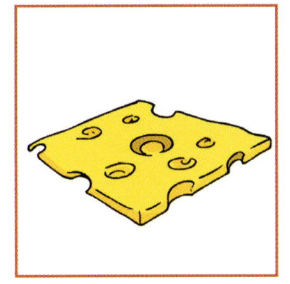

Ex. *a piece of*   a   rice
1. a bottle of   b   coffee
2. a jar of   c   chocolate
3. a bag of   d   honey
4. a carton of   e   *cheese*
5. a cup of   f   bread
6. a bar of   g   milk
7. a loaf of   h   water

Ex. *a piece of cheese*   1 ....   2 ....   3 ....

4 ....   5 ....   6 ....   7 ....

Much, Many

We use *much* with noncount nouns in negative sentences and questions.
They don't have much furniture in their new house.
Does she have much free time?

We use the word *many* with count nouns in affirmative sentences, negative sentences and questions.
There are many cars on the road.
I don't have many shirts.
Were there many people at the party?

When we ask about quantity, we use *how much* for noncount nouns and *how many* for count nouns.
How much coffee is there?
How many apples did you buy?

71

16

4 Complete the sentences with **much** or **many**.

Ex. Were there ......*many*...... birds in the garden?
1. We don't need .... money for our trip.
2. Is there .... ice on the lake?
3. There weren't .... people in the supermarket.
4. We don't have .... time, so hurry up!
5. Can you see .... bears in Russia?
6. Are there .... interesting shows on TV?
7. There are .... good hotels in this city.
8. I don't like .... salt on my potatoes.

5 Complete the questions with **how much** or **how many**.

Ex. ......*How many*...... paintings were in the art gallery?
1. .... cousins do you have?
2. .... cheese sandwiches are there?
3. .... rice do we need?
4. .... computers are there in the office?
5. .... sugar is in this tea?
6. .... furniture is there?
7. .... glasses of water did you drink?
8. .... milk do you want in your coffee?

A Little, A Few, A Lot / Lots Of

We use *a little* with noncount nouns. It means *some, but not much*.
Can I have some honey for my tea?
No, but there's a little sugar in the bowl.

We use *a few* with plural count nouns. It means *some, but not many*.
There were a few people in the restaurant.

We use *a lot of* and *lots of* with noncount nouns and plural count nouns. They mean *much* (with a noncount noun) and *many* (with a plural count noun).
There was a lot of food at the party.
Do they eat lots of rice in China?
They don't have a lot of flowers in the garden.
We need lots of actors for our play.

6 Complete the sentences with **a few** or **a little**.

Ex. ......*A few*...... shops stay open after 10 o'clock.
1. .... people left work early.
2. The report has .... mistakes in it.
3. Can I have .... chicken soup, please?
4. There's .... oil on the salad.
5. She put .... sugar in her coffee.
6. Can I take .... photos, please?
7. There are .... things on my shopping list.
8. I can wait for .... minutes.

7 Choose the correct answer.

Ex. There aren't ..... tables in the restaurant.
   (a) many   **b** much   **c** a few

1. He has ..... money.
   a a lot of   **b** much   **c** many
2. Is there ..... ice in the freezer?
   a many   **b** much   **c** a few
3. Can we have ..... pepper on our potatoes?
   a a little   **b** much   **c** a few
4. We saw ..... interesting movies last year.
   a lots   **b** many   **c** a little
5. There is ..... apple juice, but no orange juice.
   a much   **b** a little   **c** a few
6. There aren't ..... people on the beach.
   a much   **b** a lot   **c** lots of
7. Do you want ..... oil on your salad?
   a a little   **b** many   **c** much
8. We didn't take ..... sandwiches with us.
   a much   **b** lots   **c** many

Count & Noncount Nouns & Quantifiers 16

8 Complete the sentences with the words from the box.

| any | few | how | little | lots | many | much | some (x2) |

Ex. There aren't .... *any* .... keys in my pocket.
1. Can I get .... more meat for you?
2. We don't eat .... food in the morning.
3. New York City's Chinatown has .... of great restaurants.
4. I have a .... questions for you.
5. .... many people came to the party?
6. There's a .... soup in the pot.
7. Buy .... more milk, please.
8. How .... books did you read last month?

9 Complete the text with the words from the box.

| a lot | any | anywhere | bag | cartons | few | jar | little | loaf | many | no | nobody | some |

I don't go food shopping very often, but I went to the supermarket yesterday. There weren't (Ex.) *many* people there, but it was a big store with (1) .... of aisles and I felt lost! First, I looked for (2) .... fruit. There weren't (3) .... pears, but I found a (4) .... nice peaches. Then I got a (5) .... cheese and a (6) .... of bread. I didn't see ice cream (7) ...., but I got two (8) .... of milk. I also got a (9) .... of rice and a (10) .... of honey. To my surprise, there was (11) .... in line at the check-out! Then I looked in my wallet … and there was (12) .... money in it!

Pairwork

Work with a partner, and talk about what you eat and drink every day. Take turns. Ask and answer questions with *how much* and *how many*. Here are some ideas:

- coffee
- milk
- fruit
- water
- potatoes
- rice
- butter
- bananas
- meat
- vegetables

Writing

Write a paragraph about what you eat and drink every day. Use the ideas above to help you.

73

Review 4 (Units 13-16)

1 Complete the sentences with the Simple Past.

Ex. Nobody ......*arrived*...... at work early yesterday. (arrive)

1 After a few minutes I ......*remembered*...... his phone number. (remember)
2 We ......*stopped*...... at the store on the way home. (stop)
3 They ......*studied*...... all afternoon. (study)
4 I ......*wanted*...... to buy a new shirt last Saturday. (want)
5 They ......*invited*...... me to dinner last night. (invite)
6 We ......*mailed*...... the letters this morning. (mail)
7 She ......*played*...... basketball on Saturday. (play)
8 Mike ......*turned*...... the TV on about an hour ago. (turn)

2 Complete the chart.

Verbs	Simple Past
begin	*began*
break	*broke*
buy	*bought*
come	*came*
drink	*drank*
eat	*ate*
give	*gave*
go	*went*
leave	*left*
ring	*rang*
see	*saw*
sell	*sold*
speak	*spoke*
think	*thought*
wear	*wore*
write	*wrote*

3 Complete the sentences with the Simple Past.

Ex. I ......*began*...... work an hour ago. (begin)

1 We ......*sold*...... our house last month. (sell)
2 I .... up late today. (wake)
3 My cousin .... me early this morning. (called)
4 They .... a noise and shouted. (hear)
5 He .... on my chair and nearly .... it. (stand, break)
6 I .... pictures in the book. (draw)
7 We .... some fish at the lake yesterday. (catch)
8 They .... a good time at the zoo last Saturday. (have)

Review 4 (Units 13-16)

4 **Complete the sentences with the negative form of the Simple Past.**

Ex. Robert ....*didn't hear*.......... from his cousin yesterday. (hear)

1 They .... before me. (arrive)
2 My uncle .... them to the station yesterday. (take)
3 We .... you at the theater last night. (see)
4 I .... the computer in your office. (use)
5 We .... on vacation last summer. (go)
6 They .... work before 8 o'clock. (begin)
7 We .... very far. (walk)
8 She .... the telephone number in her book. (write)

5 **Complete the questions with the Simple Past.**

Ex. ....*Did you learn*.......... how to play golf last year? (you / learn)

1 .... your homework last night? (you / do)
2 .... home all afternoon? (she / stay)
3 .... the house with his umbrella? (he / leave)
4 .... to music in the car? (they / listen)
5 .... yesterday evening? (it / snow)
6 .... a suit to the party? (you / wear)
7 .... all its food? (the dog / eat)
8 .... a new job in New York? (Carmen / get)

6 **Write sentences and questions with the Simple Past.**

Ex. they / go to bed / early / last night
They went to bed early last night.

1 they / not understand / the question
....

2 she / say anything about work / this morning / ?
....

3 I / think about the problem / last night
....

4 it / get cold / at night / ?
....

5 he / sit down / take out a pen / and write a letter
....

6 we / buy this dishwasher / two years ago
....

7 I / not wash the dishes / yesterday
....

8 she / not break the cup / in the sink
....

Review 4

7 **Complete the sentences with some or any.**

Ex. You can't have ....*any*.......... cookies before lunch.

1 There isn't .... cheese in this sandwich.
2 Don't put .... butter on my bread, please.
3 There were .... ducks on the lake.
4 He didn't have .... driving lessons last week.
5 I asked for .... water but I didn't get ....
6 Can I get .... orange juice for you?
7 I sent .... postcards to my friends.
8 Were there .... famous people at the concert?

8 **Complete the sentences with someone, anyone or everyone.**

Ex. I can't see ....*anyone*.......... in the street.

1 .... told you about the party. Was it Mike?
2 .... likes the new office manager.
3 Don't go alone. Take .... with you.
4 There isn't .... in the office today. It's a holiday.
5 Did you see .... in my office before lunch?
6 .... is here. Let's start the meeting.
7 Was .... surprised by the news?
8 .... must fix this broken window.

9 **Complete the sentences with any or no.**

Ex. I'm sorry. We have ....*no*.......... bananas today.

1 I had .... idea you were here.
2 Do you have .... fresh milk?
3 There aren't .... magazines on the table.
4 You can choose .... color.
5 There is .... sugar in this coffee.
6 There were .... tigers in the zoo.
7 Is there .... news about our luggage?
8 There are .... buses after 11:30.

Review 4 (Units 13-16)

10 **Choose the correct answer.**

Ex. There weren't .... butterflies in the field.
   a much   **b** lots   **(c)** many

1 I can't see .... boats on the lake.
   a some   **b** much   **c** many

2 There was only a .... water in the bottle.
   a few   **b** lot   **c** little

3 Is there .... spaghetti in the pot?
   a much   **b** many   **c** lots

4 There are a .... of bugs here.
   a lots   **b** lot   **c** few

5 I can't see .... trees from my window.
   a a few   **b** any   **c** a lot

6 How .... salt is there in the soup?
   a few   **b** many   **c** much

7 Have you got .... fresh fruit?
   a many   **b** any   **c** little

8 She made a .... sandwiches for the picnic.
   a little   **b** lot   **c** few

11 **Put the words in the correct part of the chart.**

~~bag~~   ~~bread~~   butter   envelope   furniture   garden   ice   lion
milk   money   rice   ruler   shoe   telephone   town   water

Count Nouns	Noncount Nouns
bag	*bread*

12 **Match and make phrases.**

Ex. *a carton of*   a honey
1   a loaf of   b bread
2   a piece of   c rice
3   a can of   d chocolate
4   a bottle of   e *juice*
5   a cup of   f soda
6   a bar of   g cake
7   a jar of   h water
8   a bag of   i coffee

77

17 Adjectives: Comparatives and Superlatives

FRIDAY IS THE MOST DIFFICULT DAY OF THE WEEK. HE ALWAYS FINISHES LATE!

Comparatives

We can use the comparative form of an adjective to compare two people, animals or things. We often use the word *than* after a comparative.
Canada is colder than Mexico.
Action movies are more exciting than love stories.

To make the comparative form of an adjective with one syllable, we add the ending *-er*.
soft ➜ softer

When the adjective ends in *-e*, we just add *-r*.
nice ➜ nicer

When the adjective ends in a vowel and a consonant, we double the last consonant and add *-er*.
big ➜ bigger

When an adjective ends in *-y*, we take off the *-y* and add *-ier*.
heavy ➜ heavier

Sometimes we use the word *more* with two-syllable adjectives to make the comparative form.
famous ➜ more famous

Some two-syllable adjectives have two comparative forms.
simple ➜ simpler/more simple
polite ➜ politer/more polite
quiet ➜ quieter/more quiet

We use the word *more* to make the comparative form of adjectives with three or more syllables.
difficult ➜ more difficult

Some adjectives are irregular and do not follow these rules.
good ➜ better
bad ➜ worse
far ➜ farther/further

1 Complete the sentences with the comparative form of the adjectives in parentheses.

Ex. She is .... *taller* .... than her sister. (tall)

1 This movie is .... than the last one. (funny)
2 I'm .... at tennis than I was last year. (good)
3 Olympic athletes are .... than local athletes. (famous)
4 You were here .... than I was yesterday. (late)
5 Last month's test was .... than today's test. (simple)
6 Mount Everest is .... than Mount Fuji. (high)
7 History is a .... subject than math. (interesting)
8 My old bike was .... than my new bike. (cheap)

Adjectives: Comparatives and Superlatives

Superlatives

We can use the superlative form to compare people, animals or things in a group of three or more. We often use a phrase beginning with *in* or *of* to continue the sentence.
It is the most expensive watch in the store.
Maria is the tallest of all my friends.

To make the superlative form of an adjective with one syllable, we add the ending *-est*. We use the word *the* before the adjective in its superlative form.
soft → the softest

When an adjective ends in *-e*, we just add *-st*.
nice → the nicest

When an adjective ends in a vowel and a consonant, we double the last consonant and add *-est*.
big → the biggest

When an adjective ends in *-y*, we take off the *-y* and add *-iest*.
heavy → the heaviest

Sometimes we use *the most* with a two-syllable adjective to make the superlative form.
nervous → the most nervous

Some two-syllable adjectives have two superlative forms.
simple → the simplest/the most simple
polite → the politest/the most polite
quiet → the quietest/the most quiet

We use the word *most* to make the superlative form of adjectives with three or more syllables.
difficult → the most difficult

Some adjectives are irregular and do not follow these rules.
good → the best
bad → the worst
far → the farthest/the furthest

Notes

The words *much*, *many*, *a lot (of)*, *lots of*, *a little* and *a few* also have comparative and superlative forms.

much	→	more	→	the most
many	→	more	→	the most
a lot of	→	more	→	the most
lots of	→	more	→	the most
a little	→	less	→	the least
a few	→	fewer	→	the fewest

2 Complete the sentences with the superlative form of the adjectives in parentheses.

Ex. They are ......*the most nervous*...... animals of all. (nervous)

1 Is 8 o'clock .... time you can go? (early)

2 In the northern hemisphere .... day of the year is in June. (long)

3 It was .... gym in the city. (good)

4 Rock climbing is .... sport you can do here. (dangerous)

5 .... bed in the store was also .... (soft, big)

6 This must be .... train in the world! (slow)

7 He's .... person in the office. (kind)

8 My idea was .... of all. (silly)

18 Be Going To & the Future with Will

THINGS YOU'LL NEVER HEAR AT WORK.

WELL DONE! I'M GOING TO GIVE EVERYONE A BONUS!

Be Going To

Affirmative
I am (I'm) going to sit
you are (you're) going to sit
he is (he's) going to sit
she is (she's) going to sit
it is (it's) going to sit
we are (we're) going to sit
you are (you're) going to sit
they are (they're) going to sit

Negative
I am not (I'm not) going to sit
you are not (you aren't/you're not) going to sit
he is not (he isn't/he's not) going to sit
she is not (she isn't/she's not) going to sit
it is not (it isn't/it's not) going to sit
we are not (we aren't/we're not) going to sit
you are not (you aren't/you're not) going to sit
they are not (they aren't/they're not) going to sit

Question
Am I going to sit?
Are you going to sit?
Is he going to sit?
Is she going to sit?
Is it going to sit?
Are we going to sit?
Are you going to sit?
Are they going to sit?

Short Answers

Yes, I am.
Yes, you are.
Yes, he is.
Yes, she is.
Yes, it is.
Yes, we are.
Yes, you are.
Yes, they are.

No, I'm not.
No you aren't. / No you're not.
No, he isn't. / No, he's not
No, she isn't. / No, she's not.
No, it isn't. / No, it's not.
No, we aren't. / No, we're not.
No, you aren't. / No, you're not.
No, they aren't. / No, they're not.

We use *be going to* to talk about:

➤ future plans and arrangements.
  We're going to invite some friends to dinner on Saturday.

➤ something we know is going to happen because we have evidence.
  Be careful! You're going to drop the glasses!

We can use time expressions such as *soon, tomorrow, next week, this evening, in the morning, tonight, someday* and *later* with *be going to*.
We're going to visit my cousin tomorrow.

82

Be Going To & the Future with Will 18

1 Complete the sentences with **be going to** and the words in parentheses.

Ex. They ......are going to leave...... for Florida on Saturday. (leave)

1 Look at that red sky! It .... nice tomorrow. (be)
2 I .... a new cell phone. (get)
3 We .... at a hotel. (not stay)
4 He .... the boss for more money. (ask)
5 They .... in France next year. (study)
6 He is running very fast. He .... the world record. (break)

2 Complete the questions with **be going to** and write answers.

Ex. *Is she going to come* with us tomorrow? (she / come) ✗
    No, she isn't.

1 .... the house? (they / sell) ✗
   ....
2 .... a great player? (he / become) ✓
   ....
3 .... the check? (Max / pay) ✗
   ....
4 .... her to Las Vegas? (you / take) ✓
   ....
5 .... later? (it / rain) ✓
   ....
6 .... English classes soon? (she / start) ✓
   ....

The Future with Will

Affirmative	Negative	Question
I will (I'll) sit	I will not (won't) sit	Will I sit?
you will (you'll) sit	you will not (won't) sit	Will you sit?
he will (he'll) sit	he will not (won't) sit	Will he sit?
she will (she'll) sit	she will not (won't) sit	Will she sit?
it will (it'll) sit	it will not (won't) sit	Will it sit?
we will (we'll) sit	we will not (won't) sit	Will we sit?
you will (you'll) sit	you will not (won't) sit	Will you sit?
they will (they'll) sit	they will not (won't) sit	Will they sit?

Short Answers

Yes, I will.   No, I won't.
Yes, you will.   No, you won't.
Yes, he will.   No, he won't.
Yes, she will.   No, she won't.
Yes, it will.   No, it won't.
Yes, we will.   No, we won't.
Yes, you will.   No, you won't.
Yes, they will. No, they won't.

We use the Future with *Will*:

➤ for predictions about the future.
   Robots will drive cars for us.

➤ for decisions made at the time of speaking or to offer help.
   I'll open the door for you.

➤ for promises and warnings.
   I'll help your brother. I promise.
   Don't lift that. You'll hurt your back.

➤ to ask someone to do something for us.
   Will you mail these letters for me?

➤ after *I hope, I think, I'm sure, I bet* and *I promise*.
   I think I'll have a sandwich.

We can also use the time expressions on page 82 with *will*.

18

3 Complete the sentences with will.

Ex. I promise I ......*will call*...... you from the hotel. (call)

1. There's no cheese. I .... some from the store. (get)
2. I'm sure they .... the game. (win)
3. We .... your door this afternoon. That's a promise. (fix)
4. Food .... different in fifty years. (be)
5. I .... all the money. (not spend)
6. Not all cars .... gas in 2030. (use)
7. Sorry, but I .... ready in time. (not be)
8. I know she .... very hard. (try)

4 Complete the questions with will and write answers.

Ex. *Will you bring* .... me a glass of water, please? (you / bring) ✓
    Yes, I will.

1. .... better medicine in the future? (there / be) ✓
   ....
2. .... me a postcard from Jamaica? (you / send) ✓
   ....
3. .... a long time to find a job? (it / take) ✗
   ....
4. .... hotter? (our planet / get) ✓
   ....
5. .... in the hospital for a long time? (she / stay) ✗
   ....
6. .... the electricity bill today? (you / pay) ✓
   ....
7. .... my shirt for me, please? (you / wash) ✓
   ....
8. .... another chance to see the Olympics? (we / have) ✓
   ....

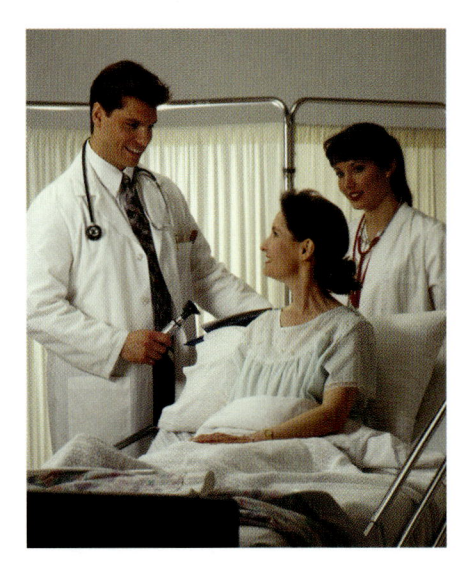

5 Read the dialogue and complete it with be going to or will.

Jack: I (Ex.) ......*am going to paint*...... (paint) my bedroom next weekend. (1) .... (you / help) me choose the paint this afternoon?

Nick: I'm sorry, I can't. I (2) .... (visit) a friend this afternoon, but I promise I (3) .... (go) to the store with you tomorrow.

Jack: That (4) .... (be) great. My cousin lives near the store and my friend and I (5) .... (meet) him for a cup of coffee at around 7 o'clock. I think they (6) .... (agree) to come to the store with us.

Nick: OK. I (7) .... (call) you after work. It (8) .... (be) around 5 o'clock. I'm sure I (9) .... (not be) late because we (10) .... (close) early on Friday.

84

Be Going To & the Future with Will 18

Pairwork

Work with a partner. Take turns. Ask and answer questions about your plans for next weekend. For example:

- What time are you going to get up?
- Who are you going to meet?
- What are you going to do?
- Are you going to do something special?

Writing

Write about a relative or friend you are going to visit soon. What are you going to do? Use the language in this unit to describe your plans.

19 Question Words

HOW MUCH SUGAR DID YOU PUT IN THIS COFFEE?

Question Words

We use question words when we want more information than *Yes* or *No*.
"Did you send the e-mail?" "Yes, I did."
"When did you send it?" "About an hour ago."

Who
We use *who* to ask about people.
Who is that man in the photograph?

What
We use *what* to ask about things or actions.
What does she want?
What is he doing now?

When
We use *when* to ask about time.
When did they finish the work?

Where
We use *where* to ask about a place or a position.
Where can I sit?

Which
We use *which* to ask about one person (or several people), thing(s) or animal(s) within a group of similar people, things or animals.
Which actor did you see first?

Whose
We use *whose* to ask who something belongs to.
Whose pen is this?
Whose bicycle did you borrow?

Why
We use *why* to ask about the reason for something.
Why did he shout at you?
Why is this water dirty?

How
We use *how* to ask about the way someone does something or to ask about someone's health.
How do you use this computer program?
How is she?

We can use *how* with adjectives and adverbs.
How heavy is that table?
How often do you go to the movies?

We can use *how many* and *how much* with nouns.
How many windows are there in your house?
How much cheese do you want?

1 Choose the correct answer.

Ex. Which / (Who) is that girl?

1 *How / When* tall is he?

2 *Whose / What* bag is on my desk?

3 *Why / What* did Sam say?

4 *Where / Who* can we stay?

5 *Which / When* do you go shopping?

6 *Who / Which* astronaut was the first person on the moon?

2 ▸ **Complete the questions with how, how much, how many, how old or how often.**

Ex. ......*How old*...... are you?
I'm twenty-four.

1 .... water do you drink every day?
About two bottles.

2 .... do you call your best friend?
Every day.

3 .... days are there in June?
Thirty.

4 .... do you spell the word "cereal"?
C - E - R - E- A - L.

5 .... is this building?
I'm not sure, but it's not very old.

6 .... is your cousin Bob?
He's fine, thanks.

Think about it

We use **How much** in questions when we ask about noncount nouns.

Subject / Object Questions

Subject Questions
When the question word asks about the subject of a sentence (the person, animal or thing that performs the action), the word order does not change.
Who broke that window?
(**Jack** broke it.)
Whose car was in the middle of the road?
(**Sandy's car** was in the middle of the road.)

Object Questions
When the question word asks about the object of a sentence, then the word order changes to question form.
Where did you go?
(I went **to the movies**.)
What do you want?
(I want **a new watch**, please.)

Notes

Do not confuse *Whose?* and *Who's* (Who is?)
Whose ball did you lose? (We lost **Tom's ball**.)
Who's in the kitchen? (**Pat is** in the kitchen.)

3 ▸ **Choose the correct answer.**

Ex. What *happened* / *did happen* at the office?

1 What *they saw* / *did they see* in the forest?
2 Who *does come* / *comes* to work first?
3 Which cat *ate* / *did eat* the chicken?
4 Where *did he stop* / *he stopped* for lunch?
5 Who *you told* / *did you tell*?
6 What *did you buy* / *you bought* last weekend?

4 ▸ **Complete the questions with Whose or Who's.**

Ex. ......*Who's*...... that man in black?

1 .... bag is that?
2 .... bicycle is in the house?
3 .... hungry?
4 .... the fastest runner in this country?
5 .... garden has the most flowers?
6 .... watching TV at the moment?

19

5 ▸ Complete the questions with the words from the box.

How   What   When (x2)   ~~Where~~   Which   Who   Whose   Why

Ex. ....*Where*.... is he now?

1 .... car is that?
2 .... movie did you like?
3 .... is she going to visit her sister?
4 .... much milk did the baby drink?
5 .... is the boss angry?
6 .... went to Spain last summer?
7 .... is happening?
8 .... did you arrive at the station?

6 ▸ Choose the correct answer.

Ex. *Which book* you prefer / (do you prefer)?

1 Which assistant *did help / helped* you?
2 Which flowers *do grow / grow* well in your garden?
3 Which DVD *did you watch / you watched* last night?
4 Which pizza *you made / did you make*?
5 Which train *does go / goes* to Moscow?

7 ▸ Match the questions with the answers.

Ex. Where is the station?   a   I think it belongs to Julia.
1   How long is the movie?   b   An hour ago.
2   When did you call him?   c   Two.
3   Whose watch is that?   d   *Near my house.*
4   Why do you go by train?   e   Fine, thanks.
5   How are you?   f   The biggest one.
6   Which table did you buy?   g   About two hours.
7   Who owns that white car?   h   My cousin, Lee.
8   How many museums did you visit?   i   Because it's faster than the bus.
9   How much sugar do we need?   j   On the table.
10 Where did you put the knife?   k   Two cups.

88

8 Write questions. The underlined words are the answers.

Ex. *Why did you wear your coat?*
I wore my coat <u>because it was cold</u>?

1 ....
I took that photo <u>last month</u>.

2 ....
I bought the carpet <u>at a store downtown</u>.

3 ....
<u>Victor</u> opened all the windows.

4 ....
The <u>yellow</u> bicycle is the cheapest.

5 ....
There were <u>hundreds of people</u> at the meeting.

6 ....
She comes from <u>Brazil</u>.

Pairwork

Work with a partner. Take turns. Ask and answer questions about your family and friends. Use the language from this unit.

Writing

Write an e-mail to a friend on vacation in another country. Use the question words *who*, *what*, *when*, *where*, *which*, *whose*, *why* and *how* to get more information.

20 Present Perfect: Regular and Irregular Verbs

I'VE FORGOTTEN ALL MY PASSWORDS!

SO YOU HAD A GOOD VACATION!

Present Perfect: Regular Verbs

Affirmative
I have (I've) eaten
you have (you've) eaten
he has (he's) eaten
she has (she's) eaten
it has (it's) eaten
we have (we've) eaten
you have (you've) eaten
they have (they've) eaten

Negative
I have not (haven't) eaten
you have not (haven't) eaten
he has not (hasn't) eaten
she has not (hasn't) eaten
it has not (hasn't) eaten
we have not (haven't) eaten
you have not (haven't) eaten
they have not (haven't) eaten

Question
Have I eaten?
Have you eaten?
Has he eaten?
Has she eaten?
Has it eaten?
Have we eaten?
Have you eaten?
Have they eaten?

Short Answers
Yes, I have.   No, I haven't.
Yes, you have.   No, you haven't.
Yes, he has.   No, he hasn't.
Yes, she has.   No, she hasn't.
Yes, it has.   No, it hasn't.
Yes, we have.   No, we haven't.
Yes, you have.   No, you haven't.
Yes, they have.   No, they haven't.

We use the Present Perfect to talk about:

➤ something that happened in the past but we don't say exactly when. Sometimes we use the word *already* or a time expression like *once*, *twice* or *many times*.
She's had a few colds this year.
She has already done the dishes.
He's been to Tokyo once.

➤ something that has not happened or finished. We often use the word *yet* in negatives and questions.
I haven't read the newspaper yet.
Has she finished the report yet?

➤ something that finished a short time ago. We often use the word *just*. (Note: We can also use Simple Past for this in American English.)
We've just arrived. = We just arrived.

We form the Present Perfect of regular verbs with *have/has* and the past participle of the main verb. We form the past participle of regular verbs with the ending *-ed*, as we do for the Simple Past. The same spelling rules apply (see Unit 13).

We put the word *not* after the word *have/has* to make the negative form.
I haven't cleaned the bathroom.
She has not started work.

We put the word *have/has* before the subject to ask a question.
Has she acted in a play?
Have you washed all the socks?

Present Perfect: Regular and Irregular Verbs **20**

1 Complete the sentences with the Present Perfect.

Ex. Natalie ......*hasn't called*...... me yet. (call)

1 The train ......*hasn't arrived*...... yet. (not arrive)
2 ......*Have*...... you ......*invited*...... Nicole and Jeff to dinner? (invite)
3 I ......*haven't carried*...... the boxes up to the bedroom yet. (not carry)
4 We ......*haven't visited*...... Brazil twice. (visit)
5 They ......*haven't studied*...... for the English test. (not study)
6 ......*Have*...... you ......*washed*...... the dishes yet? (wash)
7 We ......*have already talked*...... to the boss about the problem. (already / talk)
8 The store ......*hasn't just closed*...... . (just / close)

2 Complete the questions with the Present Perfect and write answers.

Ex. *Have they finished* their coffee? (they / finish) ✗
No, they haven't.

1 ......*Has he played*...... basketball for a long time? (he / play) ✓
......*Yes, he has.*......
2 ......*Has she locked*...... the front door? (she / lock) ✗
......*No, she hasn't.*......
3 ......*Have you cleaned*...... your bedroom? (you / clean) ✓
......*Yes, I have cleaned*......
4 ......*Has she practiced*...... the piano today? (she / practice) ✓
......*Yes, she has.*......
5 ......*Has it rained*...... much this month? (it / rain) ✗
......*No, it hasn't*......
6 ......*Have you used*...... a machine like this? (you / use) ✗
......*No, I haven't.*......

Present Perfect: Irregular Verbs

Unlike the past participles of regular verbs, the past participles of irregular verbs do not end in *-ed*.
(See the list of Irregular Verbs on page 98.)

give → gave → given
see → saw → seen

Notes

Gone and *been* can both be used as past participles of the verb *go*.

We use *have/has gone* to say that someone has gone somewhere and has not come back yet.
She has just gone to the park. She will be back soon.

We use *have/has been* to say that someone went somewhere and has come back.
She has been to Japan. She goes every year. Her next trip is in June.

20

3 Complete the chart.

Verb	Simple Past	Past Participle
be	was/were	been
break	broke	broken
buy	bought	bought
drive	drove	driven
eat	ate	eaten
go	went	gone
give	gave	given
leave	left	left
make	made	made
read	read	read
speak	spoke	spoken
take	took	taken
tell	told	told
win	won	won
write	wrote	written

4 Complete the sentences with the Present Perfect.

Ex. She *hasn't eaten* her sandwiches yet. (not eat)

1 *Have* you *written* to Ian yet? (write)
2 We *haven't made* an apple pie. (make)
3 I *haven't drived* a big car. (not drive)
4 She *hasn't spoken* to me this week. (not speak)
5 *Have* you *readed* any good books lately? (read)
6 *Have* they *gave* him a present yet? (give)
7 They *have built* a fence around their house. (build)
8 He *has gone* to Atlanta, but he'll be back tomorrow. (go)

5 Complete the questions with the Present Perfect and write answers.

Ex. *Have you seen* Big Ben yet? (you / see) ✗
No, I/we haven't.

1 .... any fruit for us? (she / buy) ✓

2 .... your leg? (you / hurt) ✗

3 .... all their money? (they / spend) ✓

4 .... a horse? (he / ride) ✗

5 .... his family? (you / meet) ✓

6 .... any work today? (they / do) ✓

7 .... vegetables in your garden? (you / grow)? ✗

8 .... his old passports? (he / keep) ✓

Present Perfect: Regular and Irregular Verbs 20

6 Write sentences with **already** and **yet**.

buy new curtains ✗
call Mr. Johnson ✓
feed the cat ✓
pay the electricity bill ✗

read the newspaper ✗
water the plants ✗
fix the table ✓

Ex. *I haven't bought new curtains yet.*
I have already called Mr. Johnson.

1 ....
2 ....
3 ....
4 ....
5 ....

Think about it

Look at the position of **already** and **yet** in the sentences.
She has already left.
She hasn't left yet.

Pairwork

Work with a partner. Take turns. Ask and answer the following questions:

➤ Have you been to another city this month?
➤ Have you played any sports this month?
➤ Have you learned much English grammar this month?
➤ Have you watched many shows on TV this month?
➤ Have you bought any clothes this month?
➤ Have you been to the movies or the theater this month?
➤ Have you made many phone calls this month?

Writing

Write a short paragraph about this month.
What have you done?
What haven't you done?

93

Review 5 (Units 17-20)

1 Complete the chart.

Adjective	Comparative	Superlative
short	shorter	the shortest
long		
good		
nice		
big		
bad		
angry		
surprised		
smart		
old		
afraid		
easy		
fit		
beautiful		
far		

2 Complete the sentences with **be going to** and the words in parentheses.

Ex. They ....*aren't going to leave*........ early tomorrow. (not leave)

1. He .... math next year. (teach)
2. She .... the plants later. (water)
3. I .... my friend this evening. (see)
4. They .... about the problem at the meeting. (talk)
5. I .... pizza again tonight! (order)
6. My friends and I .... you paint the house. (help)
7. We .... many postcards from Mexico. (not send)
8. I .... shopping before lunch. (go)

94

Review 5 (Units 17-20)

3 Complete the questions with **be going to** and write answers.

Ex. *Is she going to meet* anyone in town? (she / meet) ✓
Yes, she is.

1 .... early tomorrow morning? (he / get up) ✗
....

2 .... your new suit to the wedding? (you / wear) ✓
....

3 .... chess after dinner? (we / play) ✓
....

4 .... very difficult? (the work / be) ✗
....

5 .... for us at the café? (they / wait) ✓
....

6 .... how to play a musical instrument? (he / learn) ✓
....

7 .... any food with you? (you / bring) ✓
....

8 .... alone? (I / travel) ✗
....

4 Complete the sentences with **will**.

Ex. Televisions ....*will be*........ different in 50 years. (be)

1 Don't go out! You .... wet. (get)
2 She .... dinner for the children. (cook)
3 I .... a tip. The waiter was very rude. (not leave)
4 We .... your ring and that's a promise. (find)
5 I .... him again. He didn't say "Thank you." (not help)
6 I'm sure she .... your problem. (understand)
7 It's very late. You .... the last bus. (miss)
8 He .... here tonight. He's going to work late. (not be)

5 Complete the questions with **will** and write answers.

Ex. *Will they be* happy in another city? (they / be) ✓
Yes, they will.

1 .... time to go shopping? (we / have) ✓
....

2 .... some eggs at the store? (you / get) ✓
....

3 .... for us in 2050? (robots / cook) ✗
....

4 .... better tomorrow morning? (I / feel) ✓
....

5 .... me every week? (you / call) ✓
....

6 .... any tickets left? (there / be) ✓
....

7 .... to be more polite? (you / try) ✓
....

8 .... any difficulties in your new job? (you / have) ✗
....

Review 5

6 Choose the correct answer.

Ex.   Who opened / did open the front door?

1   Which coat does look / looks the best?
2   What did happen / happened to the computer?
3   Who did they meet / they met in town?
4   Whose dog did chase / chased the cat?
5   When does he get up / he gets up on Saturday?
6   Who found / did find my pen?

7 Complete the chart.

Verb	Simple Past	Part Participle
be	was/were	been
begin	began	
break	broke	
build	built	
draw	drew	
fall	fell	
feel	felt	
forget	forgot	
grow	grew	
know	knew	
run	ran	
sing	sang	
stand	stood	
teach	taught	
understand	understood	
wear	wore	

8 Complete the sentences with the correct form of the Present Perfect.

Ex.   I ......*have hurt*...... my hand. I can't play tennis. (hurt)

1   I .... him somewhere before. (see)
2   They .... me anything about my work. (not ask)
3   She .... to New York. She'll be back next week. (go)
4   We .... them for a long time. (know)
5   He .... all his vegetables. (not eat)
6   They .... the elevator. It isn't working. (not fix)
7   Be careful. Your brother .... the door. (paint)
8   I .... that song before. (not hear)

Review 5 (Units 17-20)

9 Write sentences and questions with the Present Perfect.

Ex. We / not send / the e-mails / yet
We haven't sent the e-mails yet.

1 they / just buy / a new sofa
....

2 He / not read / the newspaper / yet
....

3 you / write / the report / for your boss / yet / ?
....

4 Anna / be / on television / ?
....

5 I / just run / eight miles
....

6 Sonya / take / her medicine / today / ?
....

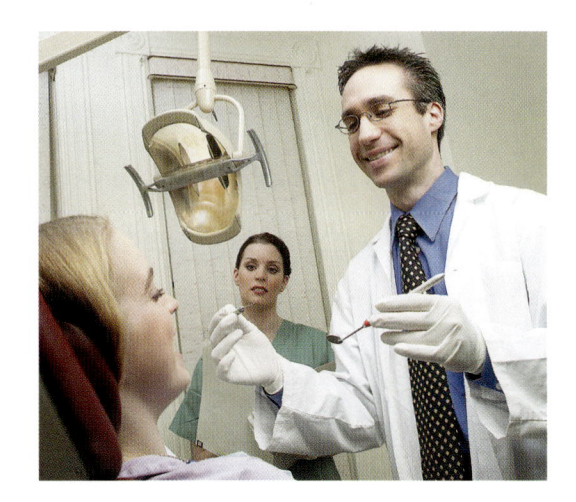

10 Complete the questions with the Present Perfect and write answers.

Ex. Have there been any phone calls for me? (there / be) ✗
No, there haven't.

1 .... which clothes to take with you? (you / decide) ✓
....

2 .... the bread in the oven? (you / put) ✓
....

3 .... which college to go to? (she / decide) ✗
....

4 .... his number? (you / forget) ✗
....

5 .... their homework? (they / do) ✓
....

6 .... here before? (he / be) ✗
....

7 .... his car keys yet? (he / find) ✓
....

8 .... the appetizers? (you / taste) ✗
....

11 Choose the correct answer.

Ex. Have you *known* / *knew* Melissa long?

1 I *haven't* / *didn't* flown in a helicopter.
2 Have you *saw* / *seen* my keys anywhere?
3 Did you *knew* / *know* Paul was a teacher?
4 He hasn't *sung* / *sang* a song in a long time.
5 Has she *drank* / *drunk* all the juice?
6 The wind *blew* / *blown* my hat off this morning.
7 I *haven't told* / *didn't tell* her yet.
8 He *has written* / *wrote* that letter a week ago.

97

Irregular Verbs

Infinitive	Simple Past	Past Participle	Infinitive	Simple Past	Past Participle
be	was/were	been	lead	led	led
become	became	become	leave	left	left
begin	began	begun	lend	lent	lent
blow	blew	blown	lose	lost	lost
break	broke	broken	make	made	made
bring	brought	brought	meet	met	met
build	built	built	pay	paid	paid
buy	bought	bought	put	put	put
catch	caught	caught	read	read	read
choose	chose	chosen	ride	rode	ridden
come	came	come	ring	rang	rung
cut	cut	cut	run	ran	run
do	did	done	say	said	said
draw	drew	drawn	see	saw	seen
drink	drank	drunk	sell	sold	sold
drive	drove	driven	shine	shone	shone
eat	ate	eaten	sing	sang	sung
fall	fell	fallen	sit	sat	sat
feed	fed	fed	sleep	slept	slept
feel	felt	felt	speak	spoke	spoken
find	found	found	spend	spent	spent
fly	flew	flown	stand	stood	stood
forget	forgot	forgotten	swim	swam	swum
get	got	gotten / got	take	took	taken
give	gave	given	teach	taught	taught
go	went	gone	tell	told	told
grow	grew	grown	think	thought	thought
have	had	had	understand	understood	understood
hear	heard	heard	wake	woke	woken
hit	hit	hit	wear	wore	worn
hurt	hurt	hurt	win	won	won
keep	kept	kept	write	wrote	written
know	knew	known			

Notes

Notes

Notes

Notes

Notes

Notes

Notes

Notes

Notes

Notes

Notes

Notes

Notes